This Stolen Land

This Stolen Land

A People's History of the Gwent Levels

Marsha O'Mahony

Seren is the book imprint of
Poetry Wales Press Ltd.
Suite 6, 4 Derwen Road, Bridgend,
Wales, CF31 1LH

www.serenbooks.com
facebook.com/SerenBooks
twitter: @SerenBooks

ISBN 978-1-78172-764-5
Ebook 978-178172-769-0

A CIP record for this title is available
from the British Library.

The publisher works with the financial
assistance of the Books Council of Wales.

Front cover illustration: Adapted from illlustration by Elizabeth Gould.
Back cover illustration: Adapted from Coloured figures of the birds
of the British Islands / issued by Lord Lilford.

'We've stolen the land from the sea. And every day the sea is trying to steal it back.'

Contents

Chepstow

Caldicot

Magor

Undy

Redwick

Whitson

Goldcliff

Nash

Newport

St Brides

Marshfield

Peterstone

Rumney

Cardiff

Severn Estuary

Foreword

Nestled between the rain-soaked hills of South Wales and the muddy waters of the Severn Estuary, the Gwent Levels have been a focus for human activity for thousands of years: the water-logged soils contain a treasure trove of buried archaeology, from Bronze Age, Roman and Medieval boats to the footprints of prehistoric hunter-gatherers who roamed the coastal marshes 7,000 years ago.

Over the last two thousand years, the once wild coastal marshes have been drained and tamed by successive generations of people, creating a distinctive landscape with a deep, rich history.

An intricate, hand-dug drainage system simultaneously protects the land from winter floods and summer droughts, creating productive farmland, and provides a home to an extraordinary wealth of wildlife. Laid end-to-end, the ditches, known locally as reens, would stretch from Newport to Rome.

Defending the Levels from the Severn Estuary's enormous tidal range is the seawall, a prodigious feat of engineering without which human occupation would be impossible: much of the Levels lies at, or below, sea level. This land may be 'stolen', but in truth it is only borrowed, and the sea is constantly in danger of taking it back.

Forming an indelible part of this rich and unique landscape are the communities that live here. This wonderful book recounts the stories of some of the people who call the Levels home; the farmers, farriers, fishermen and foundry workers, some of whom are sadly no longer with us.

Their tales are often funny, moving and occasionally poignant, reminding us of what we have lost over the last 70 years and how precious the Levels still is. *This Stolen Land* captures the trials, tribulations, and joys of living on the Levels.

Chris Harris
Living Levels / Lefelau Byw
Programme Manager

Chapter 1

This Stolen Land

'We've stolen the land from the sea and every day the sea is trying to steal it back.' The speaker is Neville Waters MBE and we are talking about Nash, his childhood home. It is February 2018 and I have been travelling from village to village along the coastal path, recording the voices of the people on the Gwent Levels for Lefelau Byw (Living Levels), a programme of work promoting and connecting people to the heritage, wildlife and wild beauty of this historic landscape.

I met Neville and his wife at their farmhouse in Caerleon. Photographs of his life, work, and family, dominate the walls. As I am led into their sitting room, a fire has already been lit. I am almost consumed by an almighty sofa, while Neville, at 86, sits king-like in his armchair. He wears a jacket and tie, old-school formality. He is sharp and incisive and talks with little emotion, though I'm sure it is there. His perspective is a pragmatic one, but it also voiced his frustration.

'It's the depredations of the sea, and sometimes the sea wins. It gets angry and knocks the sea wall down and comes back to where it belonged. But we've adapted to it here on the Levels. That's why we are almost an indigenous people and don't go anywhere else. They say we have wet feet down here.'

This is a historic landscape. To the untrained eye, that isn't immediately obvious. As one of the largest blocks of coastal and floodplain grazing marsh still surviving in Britain today, it was laid down by Roman drainage engineers, and then farmed and fished for at least 2,000 years. The official title for these flatlands is the Gwent Levels, but to those living here, the Levellers, it is often 'The Moors'. A far more evocative and apt description of a land apart, embattled, a coastal community at the sharp edge of rising sea levels. Neville again: 'What people don't understand is that the sea has made the Levels. Our friends in various places call it the Moors, because the Welsh word for the sea is *Môr*, and the Bristol Channel and Severn Estuary are called in Welsh *Môr Hafren*, the Severn Sea. The sea made the Moors and the Moors are part of the sea.'

Neville's description gets my attention and stays with me for the entire walk. It's an unsettling experience to imagine the sea above you and not below you. It came home forcefully a few days into my journey. I was at the Sea Wall tea rooms at Goldcliff. I shared a table with a wizened old man: 'When you're sat by here at high tide on a rough day, the tide is about 10 feet above you. But we try not to think about that,' he said calmly, missing the alarm in my face. 'As a boy we lived close to the sea wall bank and you'd get a good high tide coming over. It would go down the foundations of the house and through the kitchen and out through the front door. We used to have to move upstairs and light fires in the bedrooms.'

As I stepped out and looked left, there it was, looming up in front of me. I walked up the 20 steps or so and the tide was up. The Severn was lapping several feet below me. It felt ominous.

Wide skies over the estuary at sunset. Flooded reens at Wentloog under a full moon. Lave net fishermen under the Severn Bridge at dawn. Each of these places has a character all of its own. February is never a great month, but the weather is as bleak as my mood as I head for the lighthouse at Nash. I'm on a recce before I start my walk in earnest. I want to see what I have let myself in for. There are very few people around but I'm not in the mood for talking. I'm alone in my thoughts. I keep walking and can feel the bone-shuddering wind that howls off the Severn Sea, grey waters pounding, again and again. As the tide sweeps in I sense the vibrations of that relentless push (each wave weighing as much as four tonnes) as the Severn seeks to take back its hinterland. The estuary's swirling menace matches my mood. I turn away, but the scene behind me doesn't improve. It's not exactly picturesque. Through a constant drizzle, all I can see are pylons, a power station, and steelworks. I don't think I'm seeing this place at its best. *What sort of godforsaken place is this*, I mutter to myself? I'm tempted to abandon plans for the walk altogether. But, as this journey will teach me, I just have to give it time. Everything needs more time. And it is something I definitely need.

The events of the last few months have been grueling and my usual resilience and resourcefulness have abandoned me. But as I trudge on I will come to realise resourcefulness and resilience are why the Levels survive. There is only one thing for it – get my head down and get on with it.

Although it's not immediately apparent, the land behind the sea wall is rich in natural, semi-natural, and man-made treasures. Lying below sea level, it is listed as "outstanding" on the register of landscapes of historic interest in Wales by Cadw (the Welsh Government's historic environment service). There are three Levels: the Wentloog Level, the Caldicot Level, and in the middle, the Mendalgief Level, which is the piece of land between the River Usk and the Ebbw, now covered over by the city of Newport. 'The main thing they have in common,' Neville tells me, 'is they were mostly farmed until the last century, when they were built up, but still subject to the depredations of the sea. They're always at risk.'

There is a coastline here, but no crystalline beaches or rolling surf, and it lacks the sort of tourist attractions so beloved in other parts of coastal Wales. But they are here; you just have to look a bit harder. Steven Morris, writing in The Guardian (November 18th, 2018), felt moved to describe the Levels as 'so full of life that conservationists compare its diversity to the Amazon rainforest.' That is because traditional farming methods have nurtured a richly varied wildlife from the world's smallest flowering vascular plant, *Wolffia arrhiza*, to top predators like the harmless grass snake (*Natrix helvetica*) and otter (*Lutra lutra*). The 1,629 km of drainage grips, ditches, reens and rivers have also created a home for plants such as the Water Plantain (*Alisma plantago-aquatica*) with its delicate white flower, and Arrowhead (*Sagittaria sagittifolia*). Submerged plants like pondweeds, and floating-leaf plants like Water Starwort (*Callitriche*) and Frogbit (*Hydrocharis morus-ranae*), are common throughout the drainage system. The Levels remain one of the few strongholds for the Shrill Carder bumblebee *(Bombus sylvarum)*, a UK priority species, and several European protected mammal and amphibian species, and UK protected species, have been spotted, including dormice (*Muscardinus avellanarius*), some bat species, great crested newt (*Triturus cristatus*), and water vole (*Arvicola amphibius*), or the 'water rat' as delightfully described by one farmer.

Wetland birds including the marsh harrier (*Circus aeruginosus*) and bittern (*Botaurus stellaris*), both driven almost to extinction in the UK during the 20th century, are making a comeback here. I never got to see a water vole, but was delighted to spot a grass snake swimming in a reen at Marshfield.

The Levels boast the largest complex of lowland Sites of Special Scientific Interest (SSSIs) in a coastal and floodplain grazing marsh in Wales with eight wetland SSSIs covering 5,700 ha and there are rich pockets of wildlife at places such as the Royal Society for the Protection of Birds (RSPB) Newport Wetland Reserve, Magor Marsh Reserve and Gwent Wildlife Trust's Great Traston Meadows.

The soils are alluvial, rich, and fertile, washed by the sea over many millennia, the sodium of the saline seawater absorbed deep into the earth. As a farmer, Neville Waters knows the soil. His father and grandfather farmed the place before him, and his son continues to work the land: 'We have to remember,' he said, 'that for a week every month, the tide is higher than the land on the Levels. On a normal tide, the water will be at least two metres above the highest level of the land. Just think about that.'

Neville has been a member of the Usk River Authority committee and sat on the Welsh and national committees, and the Internal Drainage Board: 'Storms, of course, make a huge difference because of the force of the tide and the waves hitting the wall. There will be a breach, maybe a few yards, 40/50 yards out, and in comes the water like billy-o.' Once it comes over, he says, it moves quickly: 'It will go as fast as a horse can run, all the way across the fields, until it hits the hills. It could still happen today or tomorrow, anytime, there's no guarantee. With rising sea levels it's an ongoing battle.'

There was a time when the sea came right up to the high land: 'Look at the churches alongside the Levels: Magor, Bishton, Llanwern, Christchurch, the Cathedral in Newport, and then the ones on the Wentloog side, going down to Castleton, St Mellons: all those churches are off the Levels, but not part of the Levels. They were not placed there by accident.

'If you walk from the sea wall towards the high ground you are going downhill, very gradually. If you go from Goldcliff head, towards Llanwern Church, that's four miles in a straight line, and you probably drop down three meters. So the piece of the Levels alongside the Hills is the lowest part of the Levels and that's why it's difficult to drain.'

For all the apparent dangers, a childhood spent on the Levels could be a blissful one. Wild strawberries, water voles, otters: 'It was paradise,' Arthur Thomas says, sitting in his smart bungalow by the church at Peterstone. Ron Dupé, a sprightly nonagenarian, was once a Rumney boy. 'We lived in Shangri-la. When we were walking along, there was all types of birds singing and you could hear the insects buzzing around you. It was quite lovely. And the air. I can remember the air now; it was like champagne.'

The motorway changed things. The Levels had already felt the touch of heavy industry as South Wales became the third largest supplier of coal in the 19th century. It was further industrialised by the arrival of the railways, steel, power plants, and the need for housing and infrastructure to accommodate these increasing demands. In 1967 the first motorway edged onto the Levels with the opening of the Severn Bridge. Then in the mid 1990s, a plan was announced to extend the M4 across parts of the Levels. It acted as a rallying call to the community and the beginning of a movement to protect this area: *Lefelau Byw.* The Living Levels project aimed to reconnect people and communities to this landscape, to provide a sustainable future, and to elevate this extraordinary place and people through their stories. I found the people a feisty and welcoming group, determined to be heard above all the clamour. This was their home and they were going to fight for it, its history, its wildlife, and its survival.

As I was nearing the end of my walk, I got chatting to a passerby. He listened to what I had been doing and dropped his head in thought. After a few moments, he spoke up: 'There is an awful lot of history here... you just can't see it.

That means most people don't appreciate it. And that's an awful shame.'

Change is inevitable and while the well-managed drainage system and robust sea defences have been remarkably effective, more change is inevitable. I spoke to Dr Mark Lewis, Senior Curator of Roman Archaeology at the National Roman Legion Museum at Caerleon. I first met him at the Lefelau Byw HQ in Nash. Aside from his impressive credentials, I was interested to learn that he had grown up on the Levels at Caldicot, where his interest in archaeology began, thanks to an inspirational history teacher. 'Like Canute, we're going to discover that just standing there and commanding the sea to behave, is not going to work.

'It might be necessary to work out a rationale and a methodology for allowing the sea to take any land that it requires, and to be able to move in and out of the landscape as change continues, because the one norm is change. People tend to shy away from it, but the one fact archaeologically and environmentally, is change, so we need to learn the lessons from the past to inform the future.'

Chapter 2

Floods, fish, and ferries –
Chepstow to Caldicot

I'm prepared for bad weather. It is Wales after all, but this is ridiculous. The rain lashes down as I head out from the official start of the Wales Coast Path at Chepstow. My destination today is Caldicot, a distance of nine miles. I'm going to take my time, I'm in no hurry. I will put one foot in front of the other, and think of little else. Well, that's the plan. The truth is it's bloody miserable. But maybe The Way of Tao is fitting right now. It was my constant companion several summers before on a canoe safari down the River Wye. It was apt then and it feels apt now. If you believe, as the theory of Tao suggests, that your life is like the course of a river, then the path of least resistance is to simply go with the flow. That's it. That's what I'm going to do.

People stare from their cars as I walk through the town. This is not an ideal day for rambling, but I love being out in the elements and becoming feral. It's one of my favourite parts of walking. I'm encased head to foot in waterproofs with provisions on my back. I leave Chepstow Castle behind me as I aim for the coast and the Severn Sea. It's not long before I catch sight of some spectacular 20th-century engineering spanning this cauldron of water. My journey has begun. I can't possibly get lost, can I? I just have to keep the sea to my left, right?

I had already read in the South Wales Daily, a chronicle from 1606, an account of a tsunami down here. It seemed an extraordinary tale. 'The inhabitants of South Wales had

19

to run for their lives when they might see and perceive afar off, as it were in the element, huge and mighty hills of water, tumbling one over another, in such sort as if the great mountains in the world had overwhelmed the low valleys or marshy grounds.'

It was in January 1606 that the natural disaster of epic proportions occurred, searing itself into the collective memory of Levellers for generations to come. Some twenty-five parishes were flooded, stretching from Caldicot to St Brides, drowning around 2,000 people. It was biblical in scale and drama. There were some remarkable stories of survival and many stories of loss. Two survivors, a man and a woman, sought refuge in a tree and saw a 'Certain tubbe of great largenesse' coming towards them.' The humble barrel proved their salvation and they managed to scramble to safety in it. In another case, a mother launched her four-year-old child to safety onto a beam from the rising floodwater. The child survived thanks in some part to 'a chicken that flew up and perched beside her.' The grey waters showed no mercy, no matter one's rank or status, as demonstrated by the fate of Mistress Van, daughter of John Morgan of Wentllwg Castle *(sic)*, who was drowned at Gelli-ber, Marshfield. Sir Joseph Bradney described her fate thus: 'Moreover, one Mistress Van, a gentlewoman of good forte, whose living was a hundred pound and better by the yeare, is avouched before she could get uppe into the higher rooms of her house, having marked the approach of waters, to have bene surprised by them and destroyed, howsoever, her house being distant above foure miles in breadth from the sea.'

Flood markers at Goldcliff, Nash, Peterstone, and St Brides churches are reminders of the day these low-lying communities were engulfed by the sea. It's a sobering thought as I walk along the coast. The threat of inundation from water was always present and I'm reminded of Neville Waters' observation: 'people have wet feet down here.' But the Levels face an inundation of a different kind. Now it is the Newport and Cardiff suburbs, housing, commercial developments, and industry, that steadily encroach.

Parts of the Levels still look similar to the way they did when Neville farmed as a young man, and even further back in the 1700s and 1800s. The ditches and reens still drain the land, the fields provide rich grazing for animals, and the sea wall stands strong. There has been no major breach of sea defences in recent decades, but the ebb and flow of the Severn Sea is ever present in the minds of those who keep safe the communities behind the wall.

Visitors over the centuries have described a remote, flat, bleak, and forbidding landscape, a terra incognita, a land little noticed. They are observations I'm reminded of as I walk through these flatlands of grim beauty. The people who live here have acclimatised to the unique conditions they live under: the threat of flood from the sea, and the threat of flood from its interior.

The agricultural land here is exceptional, thanks to its alluvial soils. It is a quality the Levels share with other communities and civilisations across the world and time. Each new flood that periodically deposits new sediments at the surface, is rich in minerals like lime, potash, and phosphoric acid, providing excellent conditions for agriculture. India is one of the richest countries in the world in terms of alluvial soil, covering more than 46% of its total land area, and nearer to home, the Somerset Levels and the Fens of East Anglia, are all excellent farmlands for this very reason.

Few people know the soil here as well as the farmers. They are often generations strong and Neville Waters is one of them. 'The alluvial soils act as a natural fertiliser,' said Neville. 'It's all brought here by the sea, by the maelstrom of the huge food mixer which is the Severn Estuary. We should not overlook this: in my view, it's a national asset as far as farming is concerned and it should stay that way.'

Unfortunately, the demand for food during the Second World War, and after, forced farmers on the Levels to make changes to their age-old agricultural practices. Ploughing down here has always been a challenging prospect because of the nature of the ground and the constant battle to drain water off the land. Neville: 'If you look back to Roman times, they said their animals thrived here better than anywhere else, and so did the Normans. My own experience is the same. You get an extra half tonne to the acre of wheat or barley on that land. My vision is for it to be left alone. It was only ploughed during the war by order and yielded extremely good crops.'

Neville offered a dramatic example: 'In 1940, during the first year we had to plough, we put winter wheat in, and it came to harvest in 1941. I was four years old and I remember it like it was yesterday. It was early June, and I was walking out into this field of wheat. It was a massive field and I looked up at my father's shoulder, and there was the top of the wheat. It was like being in a jungle.'

Farmers on the Levels also had assistance from an unlikely quarter: migrating geese. 'You can't stop the birds flying in and eating some of the corn,' explained Waters who had come to realise, as he put it, that 'there's a symbiosis between wildlife and the crops and what you're trying to grow.' When wheat was planted in the autumn, it was prone to disease. 'If you do nothing about it, the disease spores, which were on the bottom leaves of the wheat, were splashed up by the rain onto the next leaves. You get a lesser crop.' The winter geese grazing the meadows halted the spread of the infection. 'When these little crowds of birds paddled about in the wheat in January, they'd more or less eat it off. It got rid of the disease. And that saved us spraying it with expensive chemicals.' Good from the conservation point of view and good for agriculture.

The seed variety, bred by Capelle & Esarez, was Ministre and, according to Waters, it yielded two tonnes four hundredweights per acre at a time when the average was one tonne per acre. Yet, although the land would initially produce an extra half tonne of wheat or barley an acre, Waters is convinced the Levels should never be put to the plough again. 'Nobody on the Moors wanted it ploughed. They all thought it was mad. But it was considered part of the war effort.'

Before I left Chepstow, I spent a few hours in the library looking through newspaper archives – one of my all-time favourite activities – and found a report from the Western Mail of June 1956. The Usk River Authority was created in 1952 and one of its early tasks was to draw up a £1 million improvement plan for the area. The '£1,000,000, ten-year scheme for land drainage on the desolate Monmouthshire Moors has been approved by the Minister of Agriculture into some of the richest agricultural land in South Wales. The project includes draining of flood-prone land,' it said. But before any of this could be done, the sea defences had to be restored and strengthened for £160,000, the equivalent of £5 million today.

The scheme included reinforcing 21 miles of sea defences from the mouth of the Rhymney River, east of Cardiff, to Sudbrook Point near Chepstow. Geoff McLeod was the chief engineer of the Usk River Authority. In his calculations for improving the sea defences, his reference point was the historical tide level recorder at Newport Docks. Based on the height of the six highest tides, McLeod added another three feet to the height marked on the wall. It was a prescient decision and has effectively protected the Levels ever since.

McLeod described the work that lay ahead in a newspaper interview: 'Parts of the old stone wall had stood for centuries – we found a Roman insignia on one stone – and were in a very weak state. The old wall was in danger of collapsing and frequently had to be patched up and there was always the threat of the sea breaking through and flooding the area behind. Given a flat surface to strike on, the waves can do tremendous damage. I have seen slabs of concrete 30 feet long lifted on to the top of the sea wall and other bits carried out too.'

I stop at Sudbrook but its little museum is closed. It's probably just as well. I am already covered in Severn grey sludge. So I find somewhere to perch and pour a coffee from my flask. From here I can see the two bridges that cross the Severn.

I recall the 2005 Martin Scorsese-directed documentary about one of the greatest American songwriters of all time, Bob Dylan. The film was titled No Direction Home, and publicity photos used an old image as the cover of the album, of a moody-looking Dylan, windswept and waiting. It was 1966 and the first Severn Bridge was nearing completion. (A second Severn crossing, the Prince of Wales Bridge, opened in 1996.) Dylan was waiting for a ferry on the slipway at Beachley to take him across the estuary. We will never know of Dylan's thoughts of the trip across the choppy estuary. But we can guess by judging the views of those who took the crossing.

The Severn Princess and King and Queen ferries, regularly carried vehicles and passengers across the Severn between Beachley, near the Old Ferry Inn, and Aust on the far side. The ferries were run by Enoch Williams and family from Chepstow. For many years they had the Royal Charter to operate the crossing service. Passengers with bicycles and motorbikes were transported on a 40ft wooden boat, until two larger steel ferries were added in 1934 and 1935, with a capacity for 17 cars. The cars had to turn sharply off the ramp onto the ferry, and then were rotated on a manually operated turntable, before being parked. The process was reversed for unloading. Scratches and bumps as cars negotiated the approach, were not uncommon.

'He was a true entrepreneur,' said Enoch Williams' grandson, Adrian, talking at his home perched near the sea wall. Nothing interrupts his view across to the Bristol side of the estuary. I've watched videos on YouTube where the water is lapping too close for comfort here, but he is unperturbed by it, even if I am.

'Enoch dreamed of creating a passenger ferry between Beachley and Aust. Eventually, it got to the point when he was able to finance the ferry with some outside help and start the service in the late 1920s. He built it up from there. When it was announced they were going to build a bridge, he started looking for other opportunities, because a ferry service there was no longer going to be viable. He eventually bought the putcher ranks [used to catch salmon] at Gold-cliff, which I ran for many years.'

Dian Tonkin observed the ferries from her estuary-side home. 'I used to watch the ferries come up the Wye every evening on the tide, from the riverbank in Chepstow. On Sunday the skipper would toot the horn on the ferry so his wife would put the coffee pot on. He would come up over the railway bank, pass my dad's allotment, and dad would give him a cauliflower for his lunch. After the ferry closed the skipper became a toll keeper on the new bridge.'

The journey over the estuary saved travellers many hours, although they were often delayed by the tide. One of them was Cardiff-born Pam Roberston. I met Pam at her bungalow later in my walk at Marshfield, her home for over 60 years. As a young agricultural science graduate in the 1950s, she worked for Marshfield Dairy producing the first-ever yogurt in South Wales – 'My claim to fame'. She was a no-nonsense type, which is just as well because she risked the ferry on her scooter. 'Sometimes you'd queue to go on and there'd only be a couple of cars in front. But if the level of the water dropped, we had to sit there for four hours. We did that a couple of times. On the Aust side, there was a cafe and a sort of a shop as well and you could buy a drink and a sweet, but [there was nothing on] the Welsh side.'

The ferry carried no freight, only passenger traffic. The journeys were not without incident for Pam. 'We went on holiday to Bournemouth once, on my Vespa, and when we came back to cross over to Wales, they put the scooter on the ferry, and it slid off and into the water. They managed to grab it, but I was terrified it wouldn't work, because it had been under water. When we got to the other side, it was okay, thank goodness. There was quite a lot of mud on the ramp. It was a bit precarious. There was no choice. Unless you wanted to go the long way round, it was how everyone got across.'

The only remaining sign of the cross-estuary service is the Severn Princess. It sits beneath Chepstow Railway Bridge on the town's riverbank, between two housing developments, close to the end of the Wales Coastal Path, or, in my case, the beginning. These days the view here is dominated by the Severn Bridge. Local newspapers reported a possible river crossing for decades. The South Wales Gazette of March 1923 announced the Chepstow Urban District Council's resolve to "Support the suggestion of a Bridge at Beachley." It took another forty years before Transport Minister, Mr Ernest Maples, accepted the tender of £1,864,534 for its construction in July 1963. The design would go on to influence bridge builders across the world.

In the 1950s and 1960s, the newly planned UK-wide trunk road system, demanded bridges across the estuaries of the Forth, Clyde, Humber, and Severn. Due to the long spans involved, it was proposed that the crossings would take the form of suspension bridges. Freeman Fox & Partners, and Mott, Hay and Anderson were appointed as joint civil and consulting engineers to construct the bridge over the Severn. They started a landmark movement. According to the Institution of Civil Engineers (ICE): 'bridges all over the world are descended from the design and engineering of the Severn Bridge.' It was quite an accolade.

One of the early workers was a local lad, John Evans, whose family first arrived in Redwick in the early 1960s. He returned to the village to live in a gorgeous old farm-house within a short distance of the sea wall. John and his wife fortified me with tea and fruitcake, as we talked.

His involvement with the construction of the bridge was serendipitous. A civil engineering graduate from Imperial College, John had been returning to see his parents one weekend when, disembarking from the cross-estuary ferry, he saw a large notice announcing: 'Severn Bridge Construction, John Howard & Company'. Sensing an opportunity, he knocked on the door: 'There were only two people there at that stage – the chap who was the agent's representative and his secretary, and they'd come from the Forth Bridge, where the John Howard company had done the foundations. A young lady asked me what I wanted and I asked to see the agent. "Well he's very busy," she said. I indicated that I would wait and after about twenty minutes or so, she came down again and ushered me upstairs. The agent grilled me: "What do you want?" I said I wanted a job and that I had a degree from Imperial College and part of my master's [degree] was concrete engineering.'

The agent pointed to a pile of papers on the side: "Those are all applications for site staff." John Evans saw an opportunity: "'Okay," I replied, "but I am here". He asked me when I could start. "Monday". That was the beginning of my career in building bridges.' But working in the Severn estuary under such tidal conditions, was a serious undertaking. John again: 'I was digging up at Tutshill to start some breakwater work there, and we worked what was called "tide shifts" so you were on effectively every 11 hours. You didn't get much sleep.'

There was some apprehension for contractors new to the Severn tides: 'When we were building foundations out here, we were making all our own concrete, but it was quite convenient to hire this stuff in occasionally, and this young chap, who was delivering concrete, was very proud to be working on the Severn Bridge. [Then] he looked round and saw the tide had started coming in, inland of where he was working. "Oh my boss will murder me!" But I persuaded him the water would remain shallow for quite a while.'

Only those familiar with the Severn's tide can appreciate how fast it moves. When you see it coming, get moving and don't delay your retreat. I take a detour from my coastal travels to meet gamekeeper, and smallholder Paul Cawley at his home in the hills above Undy. We stroll down the lanes to a lookout point, where we can see the Levels sprawled out in front of us with a view across the estuary. Over 1.95 metres (6' 5") with a full beard, Paul is a gentle giant. He wears the customary checked shirt and green moleskin-like trousers, so beloved by farming and country folk everywhere, and he walks with a swinging gait: 'You have to be very early on the tide coming in, to be able to outrun it. It doesn't matter where you are in the world, if you're in a tidal area and you see the tide has gone out, and you want to know if that tide is coming back in, look as far as you can on the horizon, and you can see a little thin black line. If that black line gets bigger in the next couple of minutes, the tide is on the way back in. If you're down there and you see that thin black line, you run.

Don't wait to say, "Oh I'll see if I can see if the tide is coming in." That will be too late. If you see that black line, you run and keep running.'

The Severn Bridge contractors had come from working on other large bridge projects, including the Forth, recalled John: 'The Tamar bridge was just being finished too, so many of their erectors came up from Plymouth. By the end of the job, a lot of people from this area had become more experienced or more expert in this kind of construction, and went on to all sorts of places.'

Back on the sea wall, I am faced with the towering redbrick edifice of the Sudbrook Pumping Station. It reminds me of the extraordinary engineering at Sudbrook, which transformed rail travel 150 years ago. Directly underneath my feet lies the lowest part of the Severn Tunnel, the four-mile-long, 125-year-old route that carries trains beneath the estuary. Interestingly, soon after finishing their work on the tunnel, sixty-five miners were recruited to drive the Khojack tunnel through dangerous rock in Baluchistan, a mountainous area in modern-day Pakistan. At 2.43 miles, it is one of the longest tunnels in South Asia. How I would love to know who these men were and hear about their experiences. When construction began on the Severn Tunnel in the 1800s, engineers discovered a natural spring and built the Pumping Station to remove the excess spring water. It was a herculean undertaking. It opened in 1886 and it is still operational, pumping out 10 million gallons of water every day. It was the fledgling railway network's most innovative feat of engineering, and once every three decades, those pumps are replaced.

The railways across the Levels have been electrified in recent years, necessitating more change to the landscape, with the rebuilding of bridges and the erection of cable supports along the lines. When the trains first arrived in 1850 they brought work, housing, industry, and noise. The main line South Wales Railway (SWR), opened in stages from 1850, connecting South Wales to Gloucester and the Great Western Railway (GWR). The SWR company amalgamated with GWR in 1863. The SWR undertook prodigious engineering work: the crossing of the River Wye at Newport, a large timber viaduct at Newport, and a tunnel under the town. The boring of the Hillfield Tunnel caused the people of Newport considerable inconvenience. The tunnel was 200 feet below the surface and, being lower than all the town wells, it drained them dry, leaving the city's inhabitants to obtain alternative supplies of water at great expense.

The Severn Tunnel, between Chepstow and the Bristol side of the estuary, was even more ambitious. It promised to shorten the distance between London, Bristol and South Wales via Gloucester, which had led some wits to label the GWR 'the Great Way Round'. The Bristol and South Wales Union Railways provided rail and ferry connections, but this was not capable of handling bulk minerals, and there was soon a move to tunnel under the Severn.

Until 2007, the Severn Tunnel was the longest in the United Kingdom and, until 1987, the longest underwater tunnel in the world. The line opened on September 1st 1886, although passenger trains did not run until December 1st, 1886. At this time, there was not a single house at Sudbrook, the headquarters of the tunnel works, but once trains started running, a small office and six cottages were erected, and a temporary line was laid down to Portskewett Station.

The railways proved to be a major employer in the Caldicot, Magor and Rogiet areas, dominating this part of the Levels for decades. Ivy James grew up in the railway town, Rogiet, but it has changed. It was the bustling, beating heart of the nearby railway marshalling yards, with many of the railway workers living within walking distance.

Ivy and I chat in her sitting room. She lives a stone's throw from the former railway hub. She is now in her 90s and, according to her younger sister, quite the catch in her youth. She's a fantastic character, straight to the point and I love it: 'My father worked on steam railways from the 1930s through to the 1960s. There were few other options. That seemed to be the only work around here then. There weren't many households, you see? Where we're sitting now, in my lounge, this was a field when I was a kid. An old chap, Old Gutsy Gleed we called him, he kept his white horse here. That will tell you how much it has changed.'

That's not the only thing that has changed on the Levels. Fisheries beyond the sea wall kept families fed, while other forms of fishing bolstered bank accounts. People have fished for salmon here since the 1600s, using traditional hand-made lave nets. Locally, there is a sense of pride that this type of fishery survives here. It is the most demanding of fishing styles, in the most challenging of environments. A lave netsman (no netswoman yet) requires considerable skill, agility, and some courage, often standing waist-deep in a fast-moving outgoing tide, while trying to grab passing fish in homemade Y-shaped nets on willow frames. This style of salmon fishing is as far removed from the quiet and meditative rod-and-line method as is possible. An old ghillie friend told me that I should drop in and see the guys at the Black Rock Lave Net Fishery, the last remaining salmon fishery. I call by on a bright, but shudderingly cold day. I was desperate to warm up.

Salmon numbers have declined drastically in recent years and Natural Resources Wales (NRW), the Welsh government-sponsored body that ensures the environment and natural resources of Wales are sustainably maintained, is engaged in several initiatives in an effort to reverse the decline. 'We must stop the unnecessary killing of salmon so that populations can recover,' a spokesperson told me.

While the NRW accepts it is an important part of the history and heritage of Monmouthshire and Wales, they insist these fishermen must adapt to the changing circumstances of this wild fish.

'We do not want to stop the fishermen from using lave nets at Black Rock, but we do need them to accept that currently, the killing of salmon is unsustainable, as other netsmen and anglers have done throughout Wales. We hope to be able to find a way to secure the future of the fishery, while protecting the sustainability of salmon stocks for future generations,' added the spokesperson.

When I met these lave net fishermen, they felt their very existence was being threatened, and they were at loggerheads with the NRW. Numbers at Black Rock are at their lowest ever, and they were working hard for its survival. They are, first and foremost fishermen, but they are also guardians of the shoreline here, observing changes in fish populations, and wildlife, and discovering items of antiquity.

Traditionally, Black Rock fishermen came from the villages of Sudbrook, Portskewett and Caldicot, and had their own expressions, skills, and seamanship. Martin Morgan is their greatest advocate. In 2019 Lefelau Byw commissioned local chainsaw carver Chris Wood to celebrate the fishing heritage of the area. He created a wooden figure of a fisherman wading through water, holding a lave net as a salmon leaps out. Martin Morgan acted as the model for the figure.

I poke my head around the doors of Black Rock HQ, the non-commercial salmon fishery, where Martin, a Llanwern steel worker by day, is perched knitting a net. He is surrounded by more of these horseshoe-shaped fishing nets mounted on poles and leaning against the walls. Sets of oars are tucked away in the corner, and newspaper cuttings, and old photographs of former Black Rock fishing legends are pinned to the walls. He doesn't seem to notice the icy wind chill and is dressed in a flimsy jacket, his head and hands bare. I am shivering in multiple layers of clothing and tempted to pull a fleece balaclava from my backpack, while Martin pours out a welcoming mug of hot chocolate, digestives on the side, and starts to share his tale.

When he picked up his first licence to fish for salmon at Black Rock, the older fishermen used traditional net frames. 'When I came into the fishing in the 1990s, they still made the frames exactly as we make them now, from willow, ash, and pine. The willow came from the reens, pine for the headboard, ash for the staff. Each fisherman would make his net and these skills have been passed down from one fisherman to the next.'

Up until the 1960s, the nets were made from hemp twine. 'It would only last for two seasons, so they would constantly be knitting [replacement] nets. There was one guy in Sudbrook, Smacker Williams, who was proficient in knitting nets. Another lave fisherman, Bob Leonard, used to tell us that Smacker could knit a net in a day and a half, but I think it was probably a family effort. Smacker would put up a bar, or a rope, in the living room and knit off that. Of course, come the 1960s, modern materials such as polyester nylon came in and that is virtually indestructible.

There are three major factors to consider when venturing out into the estuary with a lave net, and only a fool would ignore them: the size of the tide, the height of the tide, and the direction of the wind. I've watched elver fishermen working the banks of the Severn, filling their vans and trucks with bucket after bucket of writhing black creatures, and making big money, but lave net fishing is neither intense or profitable, it never has been.'

Martin: 'You want it as calm as possible when you go out

there, and the wind as light as possible. You can either walk, wade out, or take the boat. When you get there, you put the net in front of you, open it out, [and] put your hand in the net to feel for fish coming in. You are continuously scanning and looking for a fish, looking for the 'lode', the mark left in the water by the swimming fish.' The fish, often pursued along rocks and sandbanks, is scooped up in the net.

Black Rock fishermen only fish in specific spots, using knowledge that has been passed down from generation to generation. 'We fish in places with names that are only known to the fishermen: The Gutt, Lighthouse Veer, Gruggy, The Marl. Then there's the Hole, the Grandstand, Monkey Tump. These are names that don't appear on maps, but are used by fishermen to describe where they fish. Years ago, you could talk in a pub, and nobody would know what you were talking about, it was a sort of a secret language.

'It's possible people have been fishing from these same spots for hundreds of years if not thousands. We've found ancient fishing baskets out there preserved in the mud and silt.

'In my great-grandfather's day, it was a super secretive business. They were explicitly told not to talk about salmon fishing. Perhaps because of money, jealousy even, but they wouldn't brag about fishing, or wouldn't tell anyone about it. If you walked up to Doug Brown, one of the old fishermen, and said, "Any fish about Doug?" He'd probably have one under his arm and he'd still say "No!" Nobody outside Sudbrook and Portskewett probably knew about lave net fishing, that's how secretive it was then.'

Martin talks about the informal hierarchy to fishing here: 'There was fishing for white fish, of course – good free food for the table.' But for Black Rock fisherman, the salmon was king. 'Salmon fishermen wouldn't be seen dead catching white fish. A salmon fisherman was a proper fisherman if you like.'

His great-grandfather, William Corbin, started traditional salmon fishing at Black Rock on his return from the First World War. He was, by all accounts, something of a character, daring too. He grew up in Chepstow and earned the nickname Nester from his habit of climbing cliffs along the Wye at Chepstow to collect seagulls' eggs for food. Since he also regularly jumped off the railway bridge crossing the river, one can understand how fishing in these forbidding waters did not faze him.

Everyone knew his house as the informal HQ, and it was where the salmon always took priority. Martin's mother used to have to wait for her bath, since it was often full of fish. The salmon were tipped into the tin bath, before being transported to Portskewett Station from where they were put on the train to Billingsgate Market in London.

It was one of Martin's uncles who first sparked a fascination for fishing in him, a sense of adventure, a little bit of danger, the hunt: 'Two of my mother's brothers were fishermen. One was quite keen, and I'd always be nagging him to take me. So, one beautiful summer's day, he took me out onto the estuary.

'We walked from Sudbrook, across the Roman Camp there, down the foreshore and then through the mud and gravel, to a place called the Luby.' They fished the tide out and stood on top of the Camp. 'My uncle said to me, "As soon as the black stones, the Black Bedwins, start to show [above the water] that's when we start walking". I never had waders, just an old pair of boots, some jeans, and a T-shirt. It was just a massive adventure, and it planted a seed for me.'

Martin's knowledge has sharpened over the years: 'You got to know what's under the water because some areas are full of holes and gullies, and you could break a leg. There's a particular gully out there now that never used to be there. When they built the second Severn crossing, they ran a trench from the crossing to the Red Beacon on Ladybench, which is about two-foot-deep and about 18-inches wide. It has a cable running through it to take electricity to the beacon, and it's right behind what we call the Pillars, two little rocks when we're fishing Gruggy. And with a gully like that, you will break a leg if you go through it.'

But there is one thing Black Rock and the NRW can agree on: salmon fishing has declined: 'Years ago, there were more fish about, and you had more chance of them swimming into the net'. And when twine gave way to nylon, the craft of net making also started to die out. 'Net skills were not being passed down because they all had [nylon] nets. And then five, ten years passed, what happened? The nets eventually get ripped, lost and all the rest of it.'

By the early 1990s, the old guard was dying out. A new, younger generation was needed to fill their shoes – or waders – to keep this ancient method alive. Martin and his brother Richard were invited to take on the licences of two senior lave fishermen. Martin: 'They called it "Dead Man's Shoes" locally because the licence would only turn up when the licence holder was dead, and that's one of the reasons the fishery was dying – there just weren't enough people to keep it going. So, we grabbed them with both hands, cobbled together a net of sorts, and turned up one day on a fishing tide in season, gave over our money for the licence, and started fishing.

The two seniors were Dennis Lee and Bob Leonard. 'They quietly introduced us to it and started to show us the ropes. Not immediately. They check you out first, your attitude and all the rest of it. But quietly we became members of the team. Bob taught me and my brother how to knit nets, and we're keeping the skills alive.'

Chapter 3

Bombers, shunters and lapwing omelettes – Undy to Magor

Making my way from Undy to Magor takes very little time. But in historical terms the journey covers centuries. I seem to be meeting more bird watchers than walkers on this stretch of the path. I stop and chat with a couple – they're wearing de rigueur camouflage jackets and have come over from Gloucester for the day. We spend some minutes chatting about the birds they used to see down here, the lapwing, curlew, bittern and the occasional marsh harrier. But when they asked me why I was walking to Cardiff when I could go by car, I decided to be honest rather than be polite, and give nonsensical answers, as I am inclined to do so. I had been reading about mindful walking and I explained that's what I was doing. 'My plan is to empty my mind, stop the past distressing me, and forget worrying about the future, and hopefully ease some of the upheaval of recent months.' I was in full stream and ready to continue, but their faces were blank and they were twitching to go. I made a note to myself: don't bore others with your troubles. No one is interested. In a way, I found that helpful.

It doesn't take me long to reach Rogiet Countryside Park. There is little to remind the casual onlooker of the noises, smells, and industry that was here. Covering several acres, this was once one of the busiest rail hubs in the country. When the railway tracks and sidings were removed in the 1990s, nature recolonised the site, returning it to scrub and meadows full of wildlife. What great changes this spot has seen.

Driven by demand from colliery owners and ironmasters, an Act of 1845 provided for the formation of the South Wales Railway, linking Swansea with Chepstow, and thence following the banks of the Wye up to Gloucester. The new tracks made most of the level land here, with little regard for the existing landscape, often dissecting existing farm field boundaries, drainage ditches, footpaths, lanes, and roads.

The building of Severn Tunnel Junction station, and nearby marshalling yards, met the demand for coal from the South Wales coalfield, which had increased dramatically during the early 20th century, reaching peak production around 1913. That year the number of trains passing through the Tunnel was 18,099, and this reached 24,027 in 1917, equivalent to sixty-six trains a day. To meet this demand, the marshalling yards at Severn Tunnel Junction, grew in size, and covered a large expanse of land on either side of the station.

As I approach Undy, I am reminded of a story Martin Morgan told me back at Black Rock about the Royal Train.

'Bob Leonard was one of Black Rock's old timers. He taught me how to fish and took me under his wing. He told me all sorts of tales, including one about the Royal Train. It would have been the 1950s, and one day he and another netsman, Doug, were walking back from fishing at Black Rock. They were carrying two large salmon, which they had caught when, to their surprise, who should they bump into, but none other than Prince Philip himself. The Royal Train was parked up in the sidings and the Prince must have been stretching his legs. Bob said "good morning," and they had a bit of a chit chat and somehow he ended up presenting Prince Philip with a salmon.'

Painted in the claret livery of the royal household, the Royal Train was a regular visitor to The Levels. It was also the worst-kept secret by those-in-the-know-locals. Paul

Cawley's father was a policeman at Caldicot, and was often called in for Royal Train duties: 'It was deemed by someone that he was responsible enough for guarding the Royal Train. There's nothing down there now, just a piece of railway line. But it was one of those sidings where the train was hidden from all sides. And it was his job to be walking all around the embankment.'

I leave Paul and head down to the flat lands at Undy, and I am back onto the coastal path, when I bump into Albert Davies. He is quietly spoken, but with lots to say, when I tell him what I have just heard. He looks at me as if I was perfectly stupid, which, as those who know me will attest, is something I'm highly capable of. 'It wasn't a secret. Everyone knew the Royal Train stopped overnight in Portskewett. To us locals anyway, not strangers like you. It wasn't on telly saying "they're staying in Portskewett for the weekend". We thought one time the Queen would be stopping in the sidings, so they dolled the toilets up here at the station just in case she wanted to sit on the throne. As far as I know she didn't.'

Ivy James, who has lived her whole life in Rogiet, also knew when the train was parked at Portskewett: 'All the kids were down there, but I don't remember seeing the Queen or Prince Phillip. Railwaymen knew they were there, and we knew. Of course, there were their guards there.'

During the last war, when the Levels came under attack from German bombers, the government built fake railway sidings to draw enemy aircraft away from attacking the crucial Severn Tunnel Junction rail link. Bev Cawley's grand-father was caught out one evening. He was a guard on the railway: 'The false shunting yard was towards Magor Marsh way. My grandad told me he had left home and was walking up the Causeway following the railway into work, when he remembered he had forgotten his sandwiches, and so he went back. He'd just reached the house when German bombers dropped a bomb on the Causeway, right where he would have been. He was very lucky.'

Paul Cawley's mother also had a close call. Life in wartime had to carry on as usual, and shopping and errands still had to be done. She was returning from the shops in Newport, when a dog fight started playing out above her: 'She was cycling over the Moors, and she said there were bullets bouncing all along the road around her. It just so happened that the local grocer was also returning from Newport in his van, having collected supplies. He shoved her and the bike in the back of his van, and gave her the biggest bollocking of her life.'

In Rogiet, I meet Ivy James' nephew, Terry Theobald. He is a child of the Moors, and a former railway worker. I had a break from walking and he scooped me up in his car between rain showers, and showed me the sights and sounds of his childhood home. The railway marshalling yards were part of his playground. The sounds and smells of the railways still hold him in thrall, especially the year's end celebrations. 'I used to lie in bed on New Year's Eve, listening to the echo of the train whistles. It was special, because all the drivers down there at midnight, would blow them on the steam engines.'

There was no way of getting away from the railway, even if one tried to, remembered Terry. 'I would say 95% of those who live in Rogiet today, wouldn't even know the railway existed there. But in my time, and my mother's, it was a very close-knit community, because we all worked for the railways. You couldn't get away from it. Rogiet was a wonderful village to live in. As a kid, at nighttime, you could hear the tannoy echoing: "Brake van in number 8!" You could hear it all around the village. There was so much hustle and bustle, it was wonderful.'

As the children grew up, the railway remained part of their landscape of play and adventure: 'I used to love going down on the old Black Bridge,' said Terry, 'and you'd wait all day for a steam train to come along and when it was coming you'd look over, and the steam engine would come rushing through, and you'd get all the soot in your face, and then you'd rush to the other side to get the steam. My mother used to despair, because I'd come home covered in coal dust.'

It was inevitable that Terry would work on the railways too. And he started as a 'call boy' when he reached the age of 15. His job was to wake the locomotive drivers in time for the start of their shift. But he was not always welcome: 'I'd be given a card with the driver's name on it, and if that driver was due on at 8 a.m., and they wanted him at 7 a.m., then it was up to me to go up to his house at 6 a.m., and knock on his door and say, "You're wanted an hour earlier". And you'd get told to go away politely.

'But you had the other drivers, who you couldn't get out of bed, because they had got too drunk the night before. So, you'd go up, and you'd knock on their doors, and run out to the gate shouting, "You're late for work!" Most of them lived in either Rogiet, Undy, Magor, Caldicot, Sudbrook, or Port-skewett, so they were predominately local men.'

Terry moved up through the ranks to join the shunters, the gang of men who sorted rolling stock into complete trains. 'The shunters were absolutely brilliant. Some nights down on the Moors, the rain would be coming in level, blowing off that Severn, and they would all be doing that shunting and they all had sou'westers and waterproofs on.' With massive amounts of coal from South Wales' collieries coming through the marshalling yards, there were hundreds of railway wagons.

The shunters' job came with many risks. 'People got hurt; it was dangerous. You had to be on the money all the time, and have eyes in the back of your head basically. You might have a wagon forming a train to go to Margam in Road Number Three. So you would go down, and a lot of the time you would have to go underneath the wagons to put the coupling on, and do the brake pipes. In the meantime, there could be wagons coming off the hump, coming down into that siding, and bang. Several times I've been underneath, and you hear it concertina-ing, bang, bang, bang. So, you wait for it, and you used to grab hold of one side of one wagon, and lift yourself up, and then bang.

'Then you'd have the runner, a guy with a brake stick, and he would run alongside this wagon, over the hump, so it would have momentum to go down into the sidings (which were up to half a mile long). He'd put the shunting pole in, and then ride down on the pole, and when he got down into the sidings, he'd be out with the hand brake, and then down with the pole. All done by hand.'

It was a dangerous, cold and dirty job, but made bearable by the camaraderie; they were all in it together: 'Now I look back, it was the most wonderful, horrible job I ever had in my life,' said Terry, 'because it was filthy, stinking. But I wouldn't have changed it for anything.'

Terry's school at Rogiet overlooked the weekly country cattle market, and he loved to watch the horse sales: 'School was brilliant for us kids, because horses would be herded up from the trains to the cattle market, and they were sold off. The cattle wagons also came to Severn Tunnel to the auction ring here.

'It was wonderful, a proper cattle market. I can remember all the noises of the auctioneers talking so fast. Cattle, sheep and pigs used to escape, and run across the school field. There was always guys in long brown coats chasing them, and trying to get them back into market. It was hilarious.

'The Rogiet Hotel, all closed now, was a busy pub after market day and the air could be ripe,' said Terry. 'I had my first ever drink there as a youngster when I was 17 on a Saturday evening.

'At the time, they had a minah bird in the little cage in there, and it had the foulest language you ever did hear in your life. You'd walk in and it would say "eff off, eff off", and things like that.'

The market was the focal point for the surrounding farms and livestock dealers, and many farmers would drive their livestock here on foot. Ken Reece recalls the days when drovers thought nothing of leading their cattle on a five mile walk to market: 'I'd drive cattle from here, in Redwick, to Severn Tunnel market, on foot. I wasn't very old but old enough to walk it.'

Ken lives between the sea wall and the Llanwern steel works. His farm, Grangefield, once owned by the monks of Tintern Abbey, continues to interest archaeologists and historians. As I arrive, I am beckoned through the back door and in through a stone porch. Ken is retired, and as we chat over tea, he sits back bemused by my interest. It never crossed his mind that anyone might be interested in his experiences on the farm, and not those of monks who lived here a millennium ago.

His route to market used to take him past St Mary's Church at Undy, and I pay a visit to see a memorial I've read about. It records a tragedy at Undy railway crossing in 1940. Over 300 evacuees had been sent to the area, seeking safety from enemy action in the major cities. Two young girls, staying at Church Farm, were newly arrived from Hastings. Just three weeks after their arrival, they stopped to look at some beehives on their way to school. They had never seen them before. When the sisters ran back across the level crossing to continue their walk to school, they were hit by a train and killed.

Albert Davies is standing at the front door of his modern, architect-designed home in Undy. His sister is with him. 'He has so much knowledge,' she says. Their grandfather arrived from the Forest of Dean in the 1920s, in search of good pastureland. A breach in the sea wall here, left a lasting memory. 'He told me there was a high tide, and it made a hole in the wall and flooded half of Undy; it came right up to the church. The houses on the causeway, they were taking people out with a boat, out through the bedroom windows. It came right up to his farm, but never got in the house.'

Farmland like Albert's was rich in wildlife. While today's conservationists are fighting to save the dwindling bird populations through the use of wildlife reserves, it was a different picture half a century ago. Albert and Terry Theobald's childhoods on the Moors were wildlife-rich: 'It was all marshland we had here,' Terry recalls. 'You came over a bridge to get onto the Moors, and it was all flat, as far as the eye could see, all the way to the sea wall. We used to come down here, and walk in the fields for hours and hours in the spring, looking for skylark nests. There was a huge population of lapwings in the fields too; it was black with lapwings. Every spring my grandfather used to say to me, "I'd like a bit of egg, my boy, I'd like a bit of egg." Then he would say, "if you find a lapwing's nest and if there's four eggs in it, you take one. If you can get me half a dozen that would be great." I only discovered years later that it was totally illegal. He would eat them, you see? Oh, they were rich those eggs. I think it was a sort of Caldicot Levels thing for a lot of guys like that.'

Terry would be out from morning to sunset with a gang of friends, exploring the Moors and the coastline. It was a magical time: 'By the age of seven or eight, I could tell you what most birds were at a glance. The kids in our gang knew what was what. There used to be a little pond down near me, where we could see the moorhens and coots. You had all these fields with these reens, and back in the 1960s, we had bushes and reeds, where the moorhens and coots would nest.

'My job was to come down with this long net, and find a moorhen's nest with two or three eggs in it, I'd have one, same with the coots. There were that many of them, coots and moorhens laying eggs in each other's nests, you would have a coot bringing up a moorhen. Crazy place.'

With so much open water around, the boys were soon making boats. Tin tubs, and canvas canoes, as long as they floated, were used as vessels on the reens. Some were more stable than others, and accidents were inevitable. Doug Howells, who I would meet in my journey through Redwick, used to explore the reens with his friends by canoe: 'We had an old pram, and we used to push the canoe on it towards Magor and Windmill Reen. It's quite a big reen, and it was great fun.' It wasn't always a laughing matter, however. Ken Reece from Redwick, and his friend Walter, used to borrow a canvas canoe, and paddle up to the sea wall: 'But it's very difficult. It's actually easier to walk.'

Gordon Shears, a farmer from St Brides, was happy to improvise. There was always something to adapt on the farm: 'We had these 45- or 50-gallon, steel drums. We cut them in half lengthways, so they were sort of boats, and go in them, and paddled up the reens. I got too heavy, and when I sat in it, the river was near the top. I always remember thinking, "I'm too heavy for it now, I'm going to sink". But my friend went, and pushed me out into the middle, the idiot! I nearly killed him.'

Gordon can remember engineer Geoff McLeod working on the sea wall. 'Back at the end of the 1950s, when Mr McLeod was in charge, they were bringing big boulders down on lorries, and tipping them over the sea wall. But there was no roadway down here, so they brought a narrow-gauge railway to bring the materials to the wall, and the labourers carried their kit on a railway handcar. But they left it on a weekend, and us boys used to put it on the rails, and go along the track with it.'

Chapter 4

Putchers, pints and big apples
– Undy to Redwick

It's no more than two and a half miles from Undy to the Rose Inn at Redwick. From there I look across from the sea wall: Portishead and Clevedon lie on the Bristol side of the bank. In the middle, stands Denny Island (Ynys Denny), marking the north western limit of the City of Bristol's estuary boundary.

When not maintaining the reen system on the Levels, John Southall loves to fish in the waters of the Severn Sea. He lives near Marshfield at Coedkernew on the Wentloog Level, but Redwick has been the scene of one particularly scary experience, demonstrating the might of these waters. He got up to all sorts of youthful antics behind, on, and beyond the sea wall. Yet none of these prepared him for a fishing trip here. Lessons were learned, quickly: 'I'm fully aware of the perils of fishing at Redwick. It's got a lot of peat edges. You go over the wall on a neap tide, or a low tide, walk through the mud, and onto these peat edges, and fish off there. But you can only stay out for about an hour before high tide comes in. Me and a mate was fishing out there, and I said "the tide's going to be here shortly, we're going to have to think about moving soon." So, I thought we'd give it five more minutes then get going. So, that's what we did.'

John was in for a shock. 'When I turned round to walk back, the tide was already coming in behind us. We had no option but to plough through it. In places, it was up to our ankles, in others our knees, and even up to our hips. We only had about fifty yards to go, but it shocked me to get caught out like that, and I'm really careful and understand the area. If it can happen to me, it can happen to anyone.'

At Redwick, I meet Doug Howells, who was standing next to his proudest possession, a 1957 Sunbeam, bought for £125 by his father who lived here. A dapper chap in his peaked hat, Doug was chauffeur to the many wedding parties who hired him, and the car for their special occasions. He remembers the thrills when the reens froze over. 'It seemed to happen a lot when we were children in the 1960s. We used to skate on the reen that went straight across the front of our house. None of us had skates, we used to just do it in our shoes.'

Ken Reece remembers how his brother nearly came a cropper when he went ice skating in the 1950s: 'The ice can't have been thick, and he went through. Someone must have got him out and he lived to tell the tale.' Another favourite spot for ice skating was the Causeway near Undy Church, as one resident recalled: 'My mother kept a pair of ice skates under the stairs, and they came out when the reens froze. It would flood right up to the 1970s until the river authority drained the land. The winters were hard in those days, and when it froze over, all the locals would go skating there.'

The sky was clear and the tide out when I first caught sight of timbers jutting out of the mud. I assumed they were the remains of groins, but they were too tall for that. I had come off the path to eat some cheese and biscuits, when a group of ramblers passed me. 'They are the remains of putcher ranks,' they say. 'Putcher what?' I ask. I grew up on the banks of the Severn, and had never heard of a putcher before.

While salmon catches are in sharp decline now, they provided a rich bounty for most of the 20th century, and even further back. The beginning of the salmon season marked a flurry of activity as hundreds, if not thousands of putchers, were mounted up on the racks out in the river. According to the Usk Observer of September 10th, 1864, 'one occupier of putchers in the estuary took, at one tide, upwards of a ton weight of salmon in his putchers, and a draught net fisher took upwards of fifty fish in one draught.'

Putcher fishing is a traditional method of trapping salmon in conical-shaped baskets. The technique, which dates back to at least medieval times, involved stacking dozens of these woven willow baskets, putchers, into fixed wooden frames, called a rank. The rank consisted of a parallel series of tall wooden stakes, usually oak, larch, or elm, positioned across the tidal flow of the estuary to catch salmon. Fishermen went out to the ranks as the tide ebbed, and retrieved the salmon. The fish were then packed in ice or smoked, ready for transport, usually by rail. A single rank could hold several hundred putchers. One rank at Porton held as many as 600 baskets. Putcher ranks were a common sight along the Levels' coastline with fisheries at Undy, Redwick, Porton and Goldcliff.

The racks could cause problems. Mr Ralph Burge, who owned a putcher rank in the 1930s, was subject to a claim for damages in 1936 by Edward Bastion of Newport, a Severn fisherman. Bastion had lost his fishing boat off Porton in June the previous year, when it struck a stake, erected by Burge in the river, some 250 yards from the shore. Bastion claimed his boat had been holed by a stake, and he described how 'me and my companion had to swim for our lives in oilskins and thigh boots', seeking refuge on the ranks of salmon baskets.

Burge told the court that the larch poles, which held up his ranks, had lasted him thirty years: 'The wood became pickled by the salt water.' It must have been quite a sight. Such dramatics were to no effect, however, and the judgment was given in favour of Burge.

Shipping regularly caused problems for putcher fishermen. In July 1903, the SS Seagull of Manchester, bound for Newport Docks, created chaos amongst Goldcliff's putcher ranks when the crew lost control, and the ship crashed into them. Reporting SS Seagull's efforts to right itself, the Star of Gwent newspaper revealed how the accident had interrupted a lucrative season for the fishermen: 'Attempts were made to get the ship off, but without success, and eventually she drifted broadside onto the salmon baskets, carrying away several hundred of them, as well as many posts. It was a very unfortunate occurrence, inasmuch as up to the present the salmon season at Goldcliff, where Messrs E Fennell and Sons (Newport) own the fisheries, has been a record one for the last five years. It will be impossible to replace the baskets and posts before the end of the season.' It was a costly accident.

But the decline in salmon numbers has seen the end of this age-old trade. I meet Sue Waters in her Whitson home. She is a neat and poised woman, a prime mover here in heritage terms. Sue is one of several locals, who have decided to record their community's history, and have formed a very active group, the Whitson, Goldcliff & Nash Heritage Group. She used to walk down to Porton, very often along the sea wall bank from Nash, to watch: 'Mr Fennell, who owned the putcher ranks, owned a house, and every summer they would decamp from Newport – they were quite wealthy people – and bring the servants as well. My mother-in-law's family were good friends with the Fennells, and they became so fed up with salmon by the end of the summer, because they had it for most meals.

'While we were here farming, you would always go down, and bring several salmon back in the summer. Oh, the taste of a Severn salmon, there is nothing like it. Everybody in the village had salmon if they could afford to buy it. If I went down to Goldcliff, you could see old Mr Howells (a distant relation of Doug Howells), sitting on the wall, making a putcher. It was part of our village life.'

Not far from the pub at Redwick, I stop to chat with Roley Price, and his wife Anne. He's one of the few dairy farmers left on the Levels. Their numbers have reduced dramatically in recent decades, but in 2018 there were still a few, with a small concentration at Redwick, including Roley and Anne's farm. They were a great couple and Roley spoke as he found, and was very funny: 'It's quite unique really to have so many dairy units in such a small area these days,' he told me as we sat chatting. 'I've been milking or been around a milking parlour since I was a toddler, and I still enjoy milking. Dad milked cows and worked as well, and mum milked when dad was away. When mum milked, she used to put me in a cake bin because I was so small. And I'd have to stop there while she milked eight or ten cows. That's how they made a living in those days.'

This rich soil created ideal conditions for cattle. Tim Rooney's father used to run a dairy herd in the post-Second World War years at Marshfield. Tim is a farrier, still living in the same village as his father: 'I sat and worked it out a few years ago that between Rumney and Newport, below the A48, there used to be something like 40 milk-producing farms, but now there are only three. Yet they probably milk the same number of cows, because they're all huge farming units, whereas before they were all small farms, pretty much self-sufficient. Because we'd have 20 odd cows, and some sheep, some pigs, some chickens.'

Ron Perry's family farm was displaced by the power station built at Uskmouth in the 1940s. The farm didn't produce much, but what they did was enough. 'It was,' he said, 'a time when a small herd of cows was enough to sustain a family. In those days everyone down here only milked 8 to

12 cows. I mean, if you carried 15 to 20 cows, then you were in a big way.'

Roley Price's father grew up in a very different area, at Peterchurch in Herefordshire, under the shadow of the Black Mountains. Roley: 'He seemed to adjust alright, you have to, don't you? He used to pick up the milk in those days from the other farms, collecting milk churns from Nash and Goldcliff, and then taking them to Marshfield Dairy. And if somebody was late, he'd leave them behind, and say they'd have to catch up or take their milk to Marshfield themselves! He'd milk his cows, and have his breakfast, and then he'd be gone by quarter past seven.'

There's no doubt farming has changed down here. Whereas once it was subsistence, now it's often survival. One gentleman who farms at Peterstone was nostalgic as he told me: 'There was this chap up the road here, all he had was six cows, a vegetable garden, a few pigs and a couple of horses to work his ground, and he made a living. That's the difference today. He had 35 acres I think, and a family lived on that. But now it's gone the other way. I think there was 19 people milking cows here when I was young, there's only 2 now. It's frightening how it's gone, to think how many farmers were down here, small farmers, making a living. They lived like kings really, because they had their own vegetable gardens, they could milk the cows, and sell a few churns a week, and they all had pigs and chickens around here too.'

One reason small farmers managed on so little was the quality of the land. As Tony Pickup explained in *A history of the drainage of The Gwent Levels* (2015, Living Levels Landscape Partnership), 'Floodplains like the Gwent Levels are such productive farmland, because their high controlled water-tables can ensure good growing conditions during the summer months. If managed correctly, floodplain farmland is some of the richest on the planet, and is self-sustaining.'

Ken Reece had farmed at Redwick for 60 years and his farm was one of the few still managed by grips, shallow surface ditches traditionally used to drain fields. 'Nearly all of the grips on my land are intact. The only field we've drained and ploughed, is the one where we grew maize; that's the only one that's under-drained, and nice and level and ideal. You could get rid of it, but I don't think it would be a good idea, not unless you replaced it with quite an expensive underdrainage. It's summer grazing, basically. Once it gets wet, you keep off it, and you wait until it dries up in the spring before you get on it again. So, it's not rocket science.'

One of the most unusual sites for summer grazing was Denny Island, the island that sits in the inhospitable waters approximately midway between Redwick and Avonmouth. The island has few visitors, as it's inaccessible at high tide. And on a low tide, only the brave, foolish, or knowledgeable should contemplate approaching. Yet it was seen as perfect for grazing cattle.

Paul Cawley has been there: 'My relatives used to walk their cattle out there for grazing. I was only a tiddler, and I didn't really know or appreciate what we were doing. We would go off at Magor Pill, and just follow the cows as the tide went out; they knew the way better than we did. You'd see the Island straight in front of you, but then the cattle'd turn and go upstream, and then come back to the Island. There were areas of the riverbed then that were still soft sand, and the cows walked around it. I was just thinking, "where the hell are these cows going?" But they knew where they were going.

'We'd stay out there for about twelve hours. There was a little stone shelter on the island, and we'd go in and light a fire, and have tea and sandwiches while the cows grazed. Then, as the tide went back out, we returned following the cows. It was exciting getting there, because you were walking in the middle of the river. My uncles were a bit more matter-of-fact, and they'd keep busy doing something they'd brought with them to do.'

Beverley Cawley has also been on the Island: 'My grandparents lived on the Causeway at Undy, and I spent my early years down on the Moors. There was a causeway there during Roman times, which allowed you to walk through the Moors when it was flooded. That has become a lane, but it's still called the Causeway. It went all the way down to Undy, across the Moors, right down to the sea wall. I went out to Denny Island with my father when I was quite young, about five or six. There was a lot of mud, but if you knew where the Causeway was, it was still firm under foot.'

Newport-born, W H Davies, author of *Autobiography of a Super-Tramp, a Poet's Pilgrimage* (1918, A.C. Fifield), highlighted another benefit of this fertile land: fruit.

'I had taken a seat in a carriage going through the Severn Tunnel that only contained one other passenger, the carriage being in the front part of the train. I judged this man to be a gentleman farmer, and when he opened his basket and offered me an apple, saying that he could recommend it as the best fruit in his orchard – when he did this, I knew I had not misjudged him.'

Ron Dix's mother knew how to raise gargantuan apples. I met him at his retirement home in Rumney. In 1952 he was doing national service with the RAF in Nairobi, Kenya when he met Queen Elizabeth II. 'She arrived a Princess and she left a queen,' he said. 'We had an orchard in Rumney, and mother grew Laxton Pippins. They were the biggest, most delicious apples I've ever seen or tasted. Absolutely fantastic.' Her secret was to disbud the tree. 'She used to take off a lot of the buds so that the apples got bigger. Well, you couldn't eat an apple because it was so big, so we used to have one between us.'

Herefordshire and Somerset vie for the unofficial title of cider capital of the UK today, with acres and acres of orchards dotted across the countryside of both counties. But there was a time when the Levels produced enough fruit to make it a close cider-producing rival. The precious few surviving examples, are an important feature of the Levels, with some fine examples in Redwick, Goldcliff and Magor.

Much of the fruit was turned into cider, which became a mainstay of the farm worker's wage. The 'truck system', which allowed for the part payment of a labourer's wage with food or drink, continued into the second half of 20th century. It was even said that the better-quality cider produced a better quality of worker. Fruit was also taken to nearby villages, towns and markets, and sold as a cash crop as part of the farm's income. In later years, fruit was transported to Herefordshire, and processed into cider in large factories there.

Orchards on the Levels were planted in a different fashion to other counties. The planting technique was linked to the particular nature of the landscape here, and the network of waterways. When excavated, the soil from the grips, or ditches, was used to form raised ridges, creating a ridge and furrow effect. Fruit trees were then planted on the ridges to keep their roots out of the wet ground, as much as possible.

Over time the importance of orchards has waned. After the Second World War, when food shortages were widespread throughout Britain, agricultural subsidies focused on achieving higher crop yields, particularly from cereals, and a lot of small-scale fruit growing ceased to be commercially viable as a result. Increased levels of mechanisation in farming also meant reduced labour on farms, and the importance of cider as a crop declined.

'Everybody had cellars with their cider barrels in,' recalls

Sue Waters. 'Oh, there's lots of stories about cider! It was such an industry down here. The villages were plastered with orchards, all along the Severn. When you had men working for you back in the 1900s, you paid them with cider, bread, and cheese. They didn't expect wages a lot of them. They just had food and shelter. So, cider was THE drink.'

When my own parents came over from Ireland looking for work in the 1950s, we ended up in a three-bedroom house on the banks of the River Severn at Minsterworth. One of my most evocative memories of that time, was of the orchard slotted in between the road and the river. Blossom in the spring, the smell of apples in the autumn, eating wind-fall and finding worms, and Mum making endless apple pies and crumbles. That orchard has long since disappeared, as have many on the Levels.

Roley Price has witnessed the decline from his back door: 'We had an orchard full of Perry pears, but they have gone. When I came here that was a huge orchard opposite, an acre and a half almost. We had four orchards here, a couple of acres.'

Sue Waters didn't like the taste of cider very much at all: 'I can remember my friend and I, we'd be sent down the cellar to collect the cider for supper. You'd take a jug and there'd be a tap on the barrel, and you'd have a little sample before you got back upstairs. It was horrible to a child though. I can remember going to houses, and the grown-ups drinking cider with supper. You always gave the men cider. A lot of people come for haymaking, and we had what we called the tea basket. It was big, and my mother would fill it with food, and there was also cider to take down for them to drink. So, cider was the answer to everybody's needs.'

A travelling cider press was pulled by a horse and, over a few busy weeks, 'would fetch from farm to farm', as Ron Perry recalled. 'I mean if a farm had it, and we wanted it here you'd get it, and you'd be turning it all day, and then we'd be winding it down, and then drinking the cider straight out of the mill. Good stuff too. We were just kids, but we used to sip it. Ninety per cent of the farms round here made cider.'

Apples crushed, then placed in the press, and as more pressure pushed down, from the bottom gushed out a golden liquid, fresh, crisp, tangy, sweet, earthy, and strong.

Roley Price's father earned extra money going around orchards buying apples: 'Dad had a Land Rover and took it up to Usk College, and they made about 200 gallons of cider. Trevor his mate, used to be the landlord of the Rose in Redwick, and he had a smallholding. Trevor had a 60-gallon cask, and we had boys coming here in the mornings, wanting to have a drink. It was lethal.'

Farm cider proved particularly lethal, especially when it came to hay making. 'We used to have a couple of boys help, and the baler broke down once, so some neighbours helped bale. I asked "who's going to milk?" "Oh, you can milk Rol, we'll go round and haul the bales." So, he takes a bucket full of water, and about five or six flagons of cider. An hour goes by; still no bales come. Hour and a half, and I've almost finished milking by then. Two hours, nothing goes by. I finished milking, and decided to see what was happening. I goes round, and they are all fighting. They're drunk! They drunk all the cider, so we had to put a stop to that.'

Chapter 5

Bears at the fridge, Eton scholars, and fish on a bike – Goldcliff to Whitson

The cider press was kept busy at the coastal community of Goldcliff too as one resident, Margaret Gutteridge, recalled. I met Margaret at a bingo session I dropped into at Whitson's old school, now a community space, one Thursday morning. I had come off the path for a wander, and when I heard laughter coming from the hall, I popped my head around the corner. I've not been lonely on this walk, but admit I need the company of others at times. I was encouraged by the lovely ladies to tuck into the refreshments. I squeezed onto the bench next to Margaret, a neat lady with short grey hair, and a soft Welsh accent like so many down here. She's quietly spoken, and I mistook it for shyness. Once I got to know her, I realised there was nothing shy about this lady. She was gutsy and got things done. I warmed to her immediately. She remembered Melvin Jones, the cider press man: 'We used to have three orchards, but they've cut all the trees down now. We had apples, pears, damsons, plums, Cox's orange pippins, russets, and Victoria plums, loads of cooking apples, and the red apples. Mr Jones' cider press came from Nash pulled by a horse. They used to turn a wheel, and crush the apples, and then put the pulp in the press. The pressing would take a whole day, and [the press] would be there perhaps for a few days. When the cider was ready, they had casks and they were kept in the dairy. Great big casks, they were.'

Margaret developed a taste it. 'I used to love it when it was first made, because it was really sweet. My grandad caught me drinking it once. I used to go to the dairy when I came home from school, and dip a mug in. But in the end, they put a lock on the door to stop me gaining entrance.'

The Levels, said Margaret, were once full of fruit trees: 'There were orchards all over then.' In an interview recorded in the 1990s, Angela Horup noted the decline in orchards too. Her grandparents ran a farm in Nash: 'As a child growing up in the '50s and '60s, I have vivid recollections of the orchards that were in abundance in my area of the Levels. If I close my eyes now and recollect, I can see an orchard neatly laid out [in] rows, where in autumn the trees were weighed down with fruit.'

Many hours listening to her grandparent's stories, has left a clear image: 'This farm had been in my family for generations, so I had vivid pictures of my long-gone ancestors working hard to plant these very trees. It must be remembered that orchards in by-gone days were extremely important; life was far removed from what it is today.'

People depended on fruit for desserts, preserves, and a healthy diet. 'The apples [were] sold in shops because people relied on home-grown produce rather than imports. Fruit that was carefully picked, and placed in the correct storage facility, lasted well into the New Year,' she said.

You can walk from Redwick to Goldcliff along the foreshore. But if you take the lanes higher up, past Green Moor, and Bowleaze Common, the road drops down to the village, passing Whitson Court. It's a fine-looking building, with nothing to indicate its former life. As the Christmas holidays approached in December 1975, an estate car left Whitson Court heading for Caerleon. The occupants included the driver, and her unlikely passenger, a donkey. The animal had been booked to appear at a nativity event for a local school. Normal means of haulage had failed, so the driver saw no reason to cancel the booking. Instead, she used her car, and got the donkey in the back without too much of a struggle. It appeared to be quite happy, enjoying the passing scenes, with its nose pressed against the screen. Mid-way to Caerleon, however, Margaret's car was stopped by a policeman on a motorbike. He was naturally curious about the occupant. After a quick check, and probably some bewilderment, the donkey and his keeper were sent on their way to Caerleon, with a blue-light police escort. Welcome to Whitson Zoo.

Built in 1795, Whitson Court was one of the finest manor houses on the Levels. It was designed by John Nash, the man also responsible for Brighton Pavilion and Clarence House. It has an intriguing history, and a variety of residents. In 1901 French nuns fleeing religious persecution, sought refuge there. Later, in 1923, it was a school for trainee missionaries, young men bound for Africa. And during the Second World War, it was a haven for Jewish refugees escaping Nazis persecution. It was later turned back into a private home having undergone extensive restoration. But between the 1960s and 1980s, its most unlikely incarnation was that of a zoo.

Whitson Zoo was opened in the 1960s by Mrs Olive Maybury, an ardent animal lover, who provided a home to all sorts of waifs and strays, including bears, foxes, donkeys, raccoons, peacocks, terrapins, llamas, red deer, monkeys and lions. The Zoo became a popular visitor attraction, but it was Kath Johnson's farm that appealed more to one of its residents.

'Mrs Maybury was lovely,' said Kath, who still lives in her childhood home at Goldcliff. Imagine your favourite aunt, and you have Kath. She's lovely, warm, and chatty. 'I was a chopsy little girl,' she said. The local policeman used to accompany her as she cycled to Goldcliff school. 'He knew all the news, because I would be telling him all from around.

'We lived a few fields away from the Zoo. Mrs Maybury

had a deer there, and she had to keep it tethered because every time she let it go, it ended up here. No sooner had we got it back to her, then it was back again. It must have liked us. But it wouldn't stay with her, and she got fed up coming to get it.' After a mutual agreement, the deer quit Mrs Maybury's Zoo. 'In the end she said: "I'm going to give you the deer," and it never left us after that. Perfectly happy it was with the cows.'

The Johnson farm supported the Zoo in other ways: 'If you had an animal die, you would take it over to her and she'd give it to the lions. But all she had to keep these lions in what was like the old-fashioned chain harrow, the sort they would pull behind the tractor to level the ground off. We [would] hear the lion roar here, if the wind was in our direction. You just got used to [the roaring]. It never escaped as far as I know.'

The care of this menagerie became the job of animal lover Margaret Gutteridge, the lady I had met over bingo at Goldcliff. She was devoted to her charges, especially a pair of Himalayan bears. Sitting in her little front room, she entertains me with stories from her zoo-keeping days. What I found so amusing about Margaret, was how she could talk about extraordinary events, as if they were the most ordinary things in the world. The bears had been languishing in a Newport department store before Mrs Maybury stepped in. 'Reynolds store had a promotion on fur coats,' explained Margaret, 'and the bears were being used as part of the advertising. There was a hot day, and people were complaining because the bears were sweltering in the window. So, Mrs Maybury was asked if she could house them, and that's how it started. It was an animal rescue really.

'The bears were big. If they came through the door on their hind legs, they would be as tall as six feet.' On one occasion, Margaret's daughter Julie came running in the house shouting: 'Mum, Su Su is out!' Margaret went to investigate: 'There was Su Su, one of the bears, coming out of the shrubbery on her hind legs.' Unperturbed, Margaret fetched some fruit from the kitchen: 'We opened the door, and we put some oranges in there, and she went back in her den.' Su Su even attended the village school at Nash: 'I took her down in my car, the same estate car of course, with Mrs Maybury's grandson, and all of the children loved it.' Su Su stayed at the Zoo, but the second bear, appropriately named Rupert, was not so fortunate: 'Rupert went to a circus.'

Some of the zoo's other residents were more of a handful, including an inquisitive pair of sun bears. They are the smallest of the bear species, and being nocturnal creatures, tend to shy away from human contact. But they trusted Margaret. 'They were Basil and Barbara. Sometimes they escaped and got out because, initially, they were only in a temporary cage.' But Basil and Barbara were smart: 'They would go into the house, and open Mrs Maybury's fridge. They knew where to go.'

A lion cub called Jason arrived at the Zoo in a minibus, packed with children. They were from a children's home in Cheshire, where Jason had been kept as a pet. 'The children loved him,' said Margaret, 'and he used to play with them, but he was growing, and they were struggling to rehouse him. So someone contacted Mrs Maybury and she said, yes, she'd have him.'

'That was the first lion we had.' Jason became a firm favourite of Margaret's, and the Zoo's visitors. 'Oh, he was beautiful!' The young lion was also popular with a grounds man. 'Peter, one of the men who worked here, had a Land Rover, and Jason used to like getting in it with him, and riding around. But eventually, because Jason got bigger, we couldn't trust him.'

Jason finally left Whitson Zoo in a horsebox. 'It took six men to get him in, he was so big by then.' Jason was destined first for Longleat, and then to Stirling, where it was hoped he would help in a lion breeding programme.

Mrs Maybury couldn't resist coming to the rescue of any animal in need. On one occasion, she exchanged a monkey for a lioness and two cubs. An unflappable Margaret took it all in her stride: 'The cubs were Kim and Raja, and the Lioness was Olly. They had been in a circus and Mrs Maybury swapped a monkey for the three of them.' Margaret drove to Dolgellau to collect the animals 'in the back of my estate car, but we did have a dog guard. At one point we had to stop to get petrol, and it was in the days when someone used to fill the car for you. This woman was putting the petrol in and she looked in the car, and the petrol went everywhere. It was a bit of a shock. But they were very quiet in the back of the car.'

Margaret went above and beyond the call of duty for her charges, including making weekly trips to the butchers to collect fresh meat for Jason: 'I went to the butchers, Amphalette & Sons in Newport, to arrange a supply of meat for Jason. When I first told them what I wanted the meat for, I don't think they believed me.' Margaret thought she needed to prove her story: 'The next time I took Jason in the car to show them: they believed me after that.' Thereafter, the Amphalette family became regular visitors at the Zoo. 'They used to bring Jason some breast of lamb as a treat.'

It's a brisk walk from Whitson Court to the coastal feature that gave this community its name, Goldcliff. The 13th-century priest Giraldus Cambrensis referred to it as Gouldclyffe, after the bank of mica and limestone, which seems to glitter in the sunshine, hence its name, Goldcliff. In 1876 an inscribed stone was washed out of the sea wall here. It was a rough, wedged-shaped section from a square stone, and came to be known as the Goldcliff Stone. But it was its inscription, in Roman characters, that really excited people.

The translation was revealing: 'Statorius Maximus centurion in the 2nd Augustan Legion in Caerleon finished his section of the wall on time.' This records either the building of a section of embankment, or a drainage ditch by Roman soldiers of the first Cohort of the 2nd Augustan Legion, based at Caerleon, led by Centurion Statorius Maximus. It is a singular yet fascinating insight into the efforts of the Romans to keep the sea out.

They had reason to be committed in their attempts. In AD43 the Romans invaded Britain. By AD48 their legions had reached the border of Wales, and began subjugating the Welsh tribes. In AD75, after a difficult campaign, the Roman general Julius Frontinus defeated the dominant tribe in South Wales, the Silures. To strengthen their control of the region, the Romans built a fortress at Isca (modern day Caerleon), one of only three permanent legionary camps in Britain. The fortress was home to 5,000 soldiers, and contained barracks, workshops, granaries, bath houses, a harbour, and a large amphitheatre. The fortress became the headquarters of the 2nd Augustan Legion, and was in use for almost 300 years until about AD375, when it was abandoned as a military base.

During the Roman occupation, the sea wall formed a series of low embankments, rather than the current continuous barrier. As sea levels during this period were about 1.5 m lower than today, the Roman wall was probably several hundred metres further out in the estuary. Evidence of the encroachment of the sea can be seen in the stumps of trees, still visible when the tide is out. It wasn't until the 11th century that the potential of this area came into prominence again. In 1113, the Norman Lord of Caerleon, Robert de Chandos, granted land at Goldcliff to the Abbey of Bec, near Rouen in France, for the founding of the Benedictine Priory of St Mary Magdalene. To improve the land, the monks repaired and extended the sea wall along the coast towards the mouth of the River Usk, and built the network of ditches, or 'reens', to control water levels. They also rebuilt the sea wall, creating a much more substantial structure, and the current line of the wall dates from this period. By the mid-20th century, the wall was substantially raised and strengthened again, the work overseen by Geoff McLeod, the engineer at that time.

The continuous buffeting of the sea takes its toll on these defences: the pressure of each wave bearing down on them is considerable. John Southall, whom I met earlier, has lived and worked here all his life. He loves the area, but even he is unsettled at times: 'It's weird standing on top of the sea wall at high tide and looking out to sea, and then turning around and looking at the land behind. You suddenly realise how much lower it is than the sea. And let me tell you, that puts it into perspective.'

The flood defences have been overwhelmed before. The infamous flood of 1606 still forms part of the collective local folk memory here, but there are far more recent memories. Monica Howell's house is just two fields away from the sea wall at Goldcliff. She described the scene when a gale blew over one evening in 1940. Together with a high tide, it amounted to a perfect storm: 'Well, we were wellied up. I was about four, and the flood came over, and into the kitchen. It was up the step of the stairs once. That's the only time I remember, but my grandparents talked about it breaking the wall in their time, and water coming up the field in waves. My grandfather used to make his children get home in time, because he used to work on the sea wall, and knew when the tide was going to come over.'

A farmer at Porton remembered a flood in the 1960s. 'We had a tide come over, and a few fields nearest the house was covered in salt water, and that summer then, we had the best crop of mushrooms we ever had. You couldn't walk without treading on mushrooms.'

Ron Perry's family simply adapted to the risk of flooding. He makes no complaints when he describes the conditions they had to put up with. It was just part of life, and they accepted it. But his mother was less accepting. When he was a boy in the 1920s, floodwater reached the stairs of his house, putting out the fire: 'The one time we had a flood we went down to the Lighthouse, and it had taken a piece of concrete wall about a yard deep and two foot wide, and it had washed it about 12 yards into the middle of the next field. And the next morning, it was a hell of a job to get the tide mud out of the house. It spoilt some of the furniture.' The family got used to such upheavals, but his mother remained on edge. 'It happened so often, we were used to it. We used to have to put the piano on the table and the sideboard. But [the slightest noise] and Mam used to jump on the table in fright.'

Ron often made his way to school through the floods: 'We had to walk through water when the tide came over, and my father would be putting dubbin on our hobnailed boots, saying, "no boy of mine is going to school with wet feet."' The floods also had hidden dangers: 'You could be walking, and all of a sudden, down you would go into a ditch. They were filled with water, and you couldn't see them.'

One night when the flood reached the Perry's farmyard, the family had to rescue their stock, 53 sheep marooned on a bank. Roped together like mountaineers, Ron and his father set out to save them: 'We tied ropes round each other, because we didn't know where the ditches were.' They found the animals stranded on two banks of soil. 'There was a little bridge over the railway line, and dad went and brought them there. We fenced and fed and watered them until the water went down. We only lost one out of the lot.'

During the Second World War German and Italian prisoners of war (POWs), were held in camps across the country and often helped on farms. Here on the Levels, the

POWs were brought in to repair the sea wall. Mike Mazzoleni is the son of an Italian POW. I take a short detour to meet Mike at his home in Whitson.

His garden is a riot of colour, and has a water feature that attracts ducks and other birdlife. Several hours after arriving I found it impossible to leave. He is a raconteur, funny, warm, a bit outrageous. He is a mix of his Welsh upbringing and his Italian ancestry. As I left, several Wagon Wheels were thrust into my pocket to keep me going.

Mike explained how his father had been captured in North Africa, shipped to Britain, and like many of his fellow POWs, put to work on the farms. 'His name was Alessandro Valentino Mazzoleni, and he came from a place called Bergamo near Lake Como,' said Mike. 'I've got photographs of him in the desert in North Africa. They had terrible times there.' Alessandro was held in a camp at Llantarnum, and together with his fellow prisoners, sent to work at Court Farm in Whitson. He settled here after the war, marrying a local woman, and bringing up his family, including son Mike.

When the sea wall at Porton suffered tidal damage, Allessandro and his fellow POWs were sent to stem the breach. 'Prisoners were pulled off different farms to go down there and shutter off [the sea wall].' Relations between POWs and local people were generally good, but with so many men still at war, there were tensions between some of the Levellers and the Italian soldiers, according to Mike: 'It was a British/Italian thing; a bit of an argy bargy, bit of name calling on both sides. And the Italian POWs would be saying: "How the hell did you ever win a war?" Never mind the sea wall!'

Saltmarsh areas beyond the wall were famous for fattening sheep. Saltmarsh sheep fetched a premium at livestock sales. But the saltmarsh were also destinations for outings. Ron Perry used to walk out at low tide for nearly a mile from

Nash lighthouse. 'We'd have our picnics out there. Just grass it was, but it's been washed away over the years.' It was a popular playground for Kath Johnson in the 1950s. She found the saltmarsh a useful spot for watching seagoing vessels. 'We used to walk out there, beyond the sea wall. There was a lot of grass then, and you could watch the ships come into dock at Newport.'

As I learned from my Roman history lesson, the saltmarsh once stretched much further out into the estuary than it does today. Coastal erosion has washed most of it away. The old church, St Mary's, stands on land close to the sea wall. It was thought to be part of the Benedictine Priory, and the monastery fishery was one of the largest and oldest. It operated between 1113 and 1550, and it would have been a major source of income for the monks who occupied the medieval priory. Following the dissolution of the monasteries in 1541, the fishery passed to Eton College, which retained ownership until the 20th century. Fish from Goldcliff was often served for breakfast to scholars at the College.

By the 1920s, the three putcher ranks at Goldcliff held an enormous number of baskets, around 2400. But as salmon stocks dwindled, and strict quotas were brought in to control catches, putcher fishing declined and the Goldcliff fishery, which ceased operation in 1995, became one of the last to go.

Adrian Williams' father and grandfather purchased the putcher rank in the early 1960s. One of his earliest memories is collecting salmon with his mother: 'We used to take fish to the railway station. This would have been around 1965, and of course, there was no motorway then, so we would have had to come through all the lanes from Chepstow to Gold-cliff, which weren't the best then. We used to get the fish in the old Land Rover; we were probably the only commercial fishery that went to work in a Land Rover.'

When he was old enough, Adrian got involved in the family business: 'When I took over, the Land Rover became expensive, and I discovered that Renault 4s were much cheaper and did the job just as well, if not better.' As the French farmers found, you could open the back door and put anything from a bale of hay to a young calf inside. The seats were pushed down to make way for the trays in the back of the vehicle, and away you go, bring them back to the fish house, where there would be a big fridge and a freezer making ice.

'We had what we call a bosh, which is a big sink, and we'd chuck the fish in it, wash them all off, put them in the fridge, ice over them, and wait 'til we got enough to take to market. We took them to Newport Station and onto the post train in the mornings, and then they would head for Billingsgate fish market.'

The size of catches did not last: 'The number of fish that we used to catch became fewer and fewer.'

Adrian can still see the remains of the timber ranks jutting out from the foreshore from the comfort of his home, perched on top of the sea wall. When the conditions are right, this is a gorgeous spot with views across to the Somerset Levels. When we meet it's a lovely, bright day, with a soft breeze. But when it was a working fishery, there was much to contend with, especially mud. Local knowledge of the estuary helped too.

Adrian: 'A car could be driven up to the putchers out in the estuary, and check the baskets for salmon.' This was an advance on the methods used earlier this century. Horse and cart was most common, while another trusted worker, Wyndham Howells, used his push bike to collect salmon. When Adrian's grandfather bought the fishery, he inherited not just a fish house and hundreds of putchers, but also Wyndham.

Wyndham had worked for the previous owner, Newport

fishmonger Burgess, and was useful to have around. He wove the putchers from withies growing in nearby reens. His skills were recorded by a researcher at Newport Museum during the 1960s, who could see this way of life was coming to an end. Adrian: 'Wyndham would stay in the fish house repairing baskets. The fish house was a home from home for him, and repairing the baskets was an important job. He would have his sort of living area in the daytime, and have a day bed where he could have a snooze. There was a coke fire, like a pot stove, to keep him warm. He had asbestos fingers, and he used to be able to lift the top of the coke fire with his bare hands, and then he'd be able to fill it with coke.'

When Adrian first started managing the fishery, it stretched over three ranks, and every single putcher had to be checked for salmon at low tide. It was very labour-intensive: 'It was a tricky business getting salmon out of the baskets. They could be quite high, over six feet, seven maybe, it depended where the fish was. If it was on the top tier, there were rails and posts, and you'd step on the rails like a ladder. But as time went on, the number of putchers got fewer and fewer, and the price of the licence went up and up. So, I concentrated where the best fishing was, and that was the Flood, because it was always covered by water. Whereas the Ebb rank, the top row as we called it, on a neap tide, which is a small tide, would barely be covered. So, you would have no chance.

'Years ago, we used to have the Shrimp rank, which was only a small rank, and it wasn't worth putting putchers in because there were very few salmon in it. Even further back they used to use it for kype fishing.' Kype baskets are much larger, and have a much wider interwoven basket. 'The mouth of the basket is between four and five feet wide.' But these woven baskets were not selective, and would catch everything, not just salmon. He would find small whiting, flatfish, and shrimps. 'It was the first of the ranks to stop. If you can imagine going to look at it at half past two in the morning, in the dead of night, in the black darkness, it wasn't exactly the best thing to do when you had no fish in it.'

There was a lot of work to do at the beginning of the season, starting with hundreds of putchers, getting them out of storage and positioning each one on the rank. Adrian: 'It was probably three day's work, and it was as messy as anything because it's very muddy out there, and it's on peat rather than on marl. You can see tracks out there on the peat now. That's where the tractor used to tow. Every year we used to get stuck, and there would be lots of swearing and cursing, and we'd have to go and get either another tractor, or get winched in from the shore. It was a real problem. Back in the old days, all they had was a pushbike. Like a butcher's bike, with a pannier on it, like Wyndham's. He'd have to put the fish on the bike, and then he'd ride it down to the Flood, and then wheel it back with the fish on the bike. And if there was a lot of fish, he'd have to make several trips.'

At Porton, access to the ranks, was even more challenging. They didn't even have the luxury of a ladder, a conventional one at least. One Leveller remembered his grandfather's efforts. 'He had about half a mile to walk into the channel. But he couldn't have too long because you have to work behind the tides. As soon as you saw [the tide] coming in you had to clear off.

'He carried the salmon in sacks. But first he had to climb down the sea wall, [using] a series of old iron horseshoes hammered into the cracks between the stones. Sometimes these horseshoes came out in his hand. He was quick enough to grab the next one then, but he would have fallen to the bottom with his salmon.'

Chapter 6

Lost farms, angry children, and a job for life – Goldcliff to Nash

'When Lord Brecon, Minister of State for Welsh Affairs, pulls a switch at the Uskmouth Power Station, near Newport today, South Wales will be linked up with the new 275,000-volt super-grid. The development will also help the South Wales industry because the super-grid line will carry 375,000 kilowatts into the area. There will be an increased load, equivalent to the demands of many cities, when the steelworks at Llanwern begins to operate.' Western Mail, November 16th, 1959.

The Uskmouth Power Station loomed large over my first introduction to this area, and I remember it with a shudder. It was a miserable February day. Wet of course, and cold. The sky was grey, the sea was grey. It wasn't much better when I turned around. There was no pretty vista here. The power station was grim, and it matched my mood.

Suddenly an elderly man wearing a crooked hat, emerged out of the gloom. It was the only concession he made to the cold. Wearing an ancient tweed jacket over an unbuttoned cotton shirt, he was barely wrapped up. He hobbled and used a wooden staff to keep himself steady. He stopped beside me, took in his surroundings, took a deep breath, and said: 'Makes you feel glad to be alive.' And with that, he patted me on the back and disappeared into the gloom.

While the Severn Bridge has become an iconic structure, granted Grade I listed status in 1999, I wondered if the Uskmouth Power Station would warrant the same in the future.

There were two coal-fired power stations constructed at the mouth of the River Usk near Newport. The first of the two stations, Uskmouth A Power Station, was built in the 1940s and demolished in 2002. The second station, Uskmouth B, was built in the 1950s, and has been undergoing a conversion to run on biomass and waste plastic. Grass has reclaimed the remains of train tracks that still lie there, a reminder of the coal brought in directly from the Welsh valleys. But this was a very different place before power was ever generated here. Locals remember a peaceful spot, room for adventures and play, a look-out point, fields running along reens towards land's end, and then views across to Newport Docks. A tavern kept good business from agricultural workers, and passing boats and their crew. For the most part this place was quiet, just the rustle of reeds growing in reens, and birdsong. But locals don't have access to this area of the Levels now. Comings and goings are under the watchful eye of a sentry box.

A Nash boy, Glynn Vincent lives behind the church at Porton these days with his wife Anne. His hair is swept back in a style that was probably all the rage when he was a young man in the 1950s. He knew this headland well: 'I can remember, years ago boats coming up there, on their way to the docks. Sometimes they got stranded out there, and they had to wait for the tide to come up high to get out again. The boats were so close that we could chat to the stranded crew.'

Like Glynn, Sue Waters also played here. 'We were allowed to roam freely as children.' In the 1950s, she remembers the local bobby predicting the demise of this little community: 'Mr Harrison, our policeman, said to my mother, "Well Mrs Collingbourne, this will be the end of the village as we know it. When this power station's built, nothing will ever be the same here again."' He was right. During its construction, everything had to come through the village, and suddenly it wasn't safe for children to roam anymore. 'In the early fifties there was one lorry perhaps every five minutes going down that road past us, full of black coal, ash-like type, and if they swung round our bend quickly, you'd end up with a lot of this stuff over the road.'

Farmfield Lane leads from Nash down towards the river Usk before swinging back around west, towards the RSPB's Newport Wetlands reserve. Sue thinks back to the days when these lanes were virtually traffic-free: 'We children spent a lot of time going down Farmfield Lane near the power station. There were all these little lanes, and we knew the people who lived at the bottom of them, we were all friends. And the mothers were all very friendly because there was nobody else, and so you brought up your children together, and you walked into each other's houses without a by-your-leave really.

'And there were little old farmhouses, because all that area was farmed. There were the Williamses, and the Bassetts, and various other families. And places like Cold Harbour Farm, Little Farm, Red Barn Farm, all these houses were there, with quite large families. Mrs Hogg lived in Spytty Farm there, and then there was Upper Lakes Farm, knocked down to put up Aldi's, then they knocked Bryngwyn Farm down to [build] Lliswerry School. I remember farming there with my friend Elizabeth, whose family had Bryngwyn Farm, and it went right up to where Tesco is. All that area was farmed. But of course, they all had to go, and they were all erased when the power station went up.'

There was a wharf at the lookout point, which was used to assist in the construction of the power station: 'Boats used to come in all the time, come up to the wharf and tie up. It was so close to the docks in Newport, it was just across the river, so that when anything happened down there, people would flock down to have a look.'

One memorable event was the launch of Lord Tredegar's

new steam yacht, Liberty, before the First World War. It was a big attraction for people from Nash. On August 4th 1914, the country at war with Germany, Lord Tredegar wired the Admiralty, offering to place the Liberty at its disposal, as a hospital ship. The offer was immediately accepted, and his Lordship was given the command, with a commission as lieutenant Royal Naval Reserve on the hospital ship.

Also close to the old wharf was Powder House Point on the west side of Afon Wysg, the River Usk. 'During the Napoleonic Wars in the late 1700s, the ammunition and the gunpowder were all stored in these powder houses on the wharf. And there was a little place called the Wind Bound Tavern right next to the Powder Houses.' Sue points to other lost names, and places, river inlets [like] Thieves' Pill and St Julian's Pill – 'they had to have reasons why they're called that. Now,' she says, 'there's nothing left.'

The change in the landscape, so much a part of her child-hood roaming, pains Sue. 'It breaks my heart when I look back, and see how they just bulldozed our village out of memory. When the power station came initially, they hadn't taken a huge tract of land. So, we had access right up to the fence around it. And then of course they needed to buy, or compulsorily purchase, all the land around it for ash ponds.' The creep of industry edged farming families out: 'Then it became out of bounds to us, and there were these huge high fences. These ash ponds were like quicksand, and were probably 20 feet above ground level, and they would fill them with this stuff that came out of the power station, just ash. That is why, when you come out of the Wetlands, you go up this huge slope, because that was where the ash ponds were, probably hundreds of acres.'

Finally Farm Field itself was taken for development: 'Eventually they bought up Farm Field [and] demolished the farmhouse to put in the ash ponds. Farm Field had been there for hundreds of years, and it was a beautiful house, absolutely beautiful. It was our playground for many years.'

Farmfield Lane leads to Fish House Lane, and on the west side of the RSPB Visitors' Centre, Perry Lane. This is where Ron Perry was raised. His family home was at the centre of the power station development: 'I was born in a big old farmhouse, just off Perry Lane, with my two sisters. Dad farmed there until he was 83. When he passed away I took over.

'But then the power station decided they wanted to put an ash pond on the land, and the old house was pulled down. We lost 500 acres in all. They closed the footpath from the church down to the riverbank. Anyone who walked on it, went through like quicksand, and you would never be found, it was that thick. They took the topsoil off, and put in banks, about 12 or 14 feet high, and pumped ash and water into these ponds, pond after pond; they were about 12 or 14 acres at a time. We were a bit upset about it, there's no doubt about that.'

But, with industry booming, there was a huge demand for this extra power. Plans had been announced for a cutting-edge steelworks plant, on the back fen of the Caldicot Levels. The plant would dominate the landscape, a behemoth in these flatlands, casting a shadow on farmland. The steelworks opened in 1962, and employed more than 13,000 workers and contractors. The impact on local people was huge. 'Before the steelworks came, this was all moorland,' one Llanwern farmer told me.

I had come off the sea wall seeking some shelter from the wind at Redwick, and was preparing to eat, drink, and sleep, in that order. But when a farmer approached, I assumed I would be moved on. Instead, he was just another chatty local. I met so many on this walk. None of them had any idea how much these chance encounters buoyed me up. His cheeks were burnt red, a lifetime spent outside. And I noticed his hands, they were enormous. Underneath bushy eyebrows, were bright blue eyes. A collie dog sat at his heels. 'We used to play over there, bird nesting that sort of thing. It was a massive deal when the steelworks came, massive.' After he left, I took a fresh look at my surroundings. It felt so rural. But as I stood on the sea wall looking inland, the outline of the steelworks could not be missed. It dominated the skyline.

Sitting beside a reen at Redwick, is a blissful experience in early spring. It's all farmland here. There is a set of ancient barns, and the bare remains of an orchard. It feels very rural, apart from a line of trees concealing the giant steelworks.

I met Mike George at his home in Llanwern village. He comes from a farming family whose land was swept up in the steel works development. I found the route to Mike's home so curious. Twisting country lanes approach it from one direction, while another road leads onto the dual carriageway. The lane that once cut right through to Goldcliff, was blocked decades ago. And the old railway line is mere metres from his home. But, cast your eyes upwards and you catch sight of something else: we are directly behind the steelworks. His grandparents owned land in the village of Llanwern, where the steelworks was to be built: 'We kept sheep there. Someone came around to make an offer for it. My grandmother wouldn't take it. But in the end, my dad convinced her that they would compulsorily purchase it anyway, so they lost the land on that side of the railway line.'

The site was chosen by Richard Thomas & Baldwins Ltd (or better known to many as Rag, Tag and Bobtail), in the late 1950s. It was officially opened in 1962 by HM Queen Elizabeth, and Llanwern started production the same year. At the time this facility was considered an innovative manufacturing site: it was the first oxygen-blown integrated steelworks in Britain, and the hot strip mill pioneered the first successful use of a computer for complete mill control.

Like the medieval church at Llanwern, which is buttressed for stability on this marshy ground, the steelworks demanded similar support, but on a far, far greater scale. Around two million tonnes of shale were put down to stabilise this boggy site, carried in by lorry after lorry, careering through Newport, and across the Levels.

'There was a horrible feeling that everything started to change,' said Sue Waters, 'and we had no control whatsoever. Because it was very poor land, virtually bog, we called it the Bottoms, just full of old rushes. Whether it could have been used with modern farming methods, been made more productive, we do not know, but it was an ideal site for the steelworks.' However, she says, they hadn't expected the steelworks to swallow up so much of their community and its infrastructure: 'What we didn't know was how far it would encroach into our village, and take away railway stations, our lanes, our roads, and our access to other villages.

'Llanwern was the main station for us. My husband David always rode his bike there, to catch his train to school in Newport. And during the First World War and previous to that, the trains would draw up there, and all the feed for the animals would come into the village, the coal would come into the village.'

While coal came into the station, hay for the horses went out: 'David said his father would take his horse and cart up to Llanwern, and collect all the coal for the winter, and they sent all the fodder for the pit ponies in the First World War out by train from there. So, it was very important to the rural way of life here. But the works took the end of the village off, took all the green lane system out, the whole lot, and knocked down some of the most beautiful farms in the process. And people wonder why we're protective of our area.

'We had caravan sites put up to accommodate workers, and their families, our schools filled up. Nash School was overwhelmed. They had to bring in portable buildings. The worst [part] was going to school in Newport. We would catch the bus, and within ten minutes of getting on, it would be stationary and crawling for an hour, and then we would miss our convent bus because there were so many shale lorries, and you only had one bridge in Newport then.'

Angela Horup's school bus travelled from Nash to Langstone, straight through the middle of the steelworks' construction site: 'We went along Monk's Ditch and over the level crossing at Llanwern. It was a dreadful upheaval for the area. It was really and truly the saddest time of my life to see the countryside disappearing. Even as a child I felt very angry.'

There were, however, many who were happy to see the steelworks. The offer of a good salary and guaranteed work, attracted thousands to the area. Bob Dowsell was one of them: 'I've watched everything, the Industrial Road as we call it, between the Coldra and Spytty, I've watched that being built, I watched Llanwern being built. I lived opposite Hartridge School, so we had a bird's eye view.'

Bob was talking to me at his home, a few yards down the road from what remains of the old Whitson Village Hall. He is not a native of the Levels, but he has been visiting the area since he was a child. 'My dad, Harold, though everyone called him Archie, used to drive for Llanwern Slag, and delivered shale to the site, when it was going into the foundation for the steelworks. He was brought up off the Corporation Road, and worked at Stewarts & Lloyds from the age of thirteen as a sheet passer, so basically, he was in the steel industry from that age and my grandfather, Charlie Dowsell, was a night watchman when the steelworks was being built. I can remember taking him sandwiches when he was working – must have been around 1959.'

Mike George's grandparents may have lost land to the steelwork's development, but his father also spotted an opportunity: 'Barn Farm was his first venture with a little caravan park for the boys working on the steelworks.' His father also kept busy running a fleet of shale lorries: 'I used to walk over there with my dad when they were piling, and as they pushed the piles in, you used to get the clay, and all the stinking mud come up the side of the piles. It was like a moonscape over there, and it frightened me to death. They basically flattened it, and filled it with stone.'

The narrow road outside Ken Reece's farm in Redwick, caused difficulties for the shale lorry drivers. Ken was often called on for help: 'They used to come off the road here regularly. If I had one bloke come in here and say "can you pull us out?" then I've had dozens. The shale lorries were one of the biggest problems. When you think that the whole of the steelworks must have been built on at least four feet of shale and stuff, that's a hell of a lot to bring in, and it was all on lorries coming through the villages here.'

Farm workers in fields nearby, felt the vibrations as the pilings went in. Paul Cawley: 'They had to put so much down to compress the peat enough to do that. When they were building, we were cutting hay two fields away, and you could feel the ground moving under your feet. The road was shaking because basically, you're on a massive platform of peat.'

There were objections to this constant stream of dusty traffic, but it was progress, said Tony Rodriguez. Tony was 23 years old, when he saw an advertisement for engineers at Llanwern in the late 1950s. It was, he said, a very exciting, and progressive operation for its time. When I met Tony, 90, I ask him how a Welshman ends up with a surname like

Rodriguez. He told me his grandfather, Paul Rodriguez, was an American ship's carpenter, and that when his vessel moored at Newport in the early 1900s, the skipper and crew took lodgings for a few days in a hotel by the Custom House. It was run by an Irish lady from Donegal, Agnes Duggan. The couple fell in love, and Paul never saw the States again.

Tony had secured a job at Llanwern. 'It was the first steelworks in the world to rely on top-blown oxygen to create the steel. Before that, it was either the Bessemer vessel or open-hearth furnaces, which were very costly to operate. A huge labour force was required to erect the works. And then you had a camp up the road at Nash on Pye Corner with all the Irish men. There was even a church for the Irishmen. They were the main ones on the steelworks. They'd go to a town on a Friday night, come home all drunk, and the priests would be collecting them up.

'Of course, with all these people coming down they needed accommodation too. I used to take people that came from Ebbw Vale who wanted a job, to show them the council-built houses at Llanmartin and Risca and in Newport. Most of them were living in little terraced houses, so when they saw the brand-new semi-detached houses, they thought [it was] marvellous.'

The steelworks also employed several generations of the same families. Many workers went in as apprentices. Mike Mazzoleni was one, following his father, who also worked there: 'There were thousands of people employed. There was so much work in Newport then, not just Llanwern. There was the docks, Whiteheads, Lysaght's, Alfra Steel. And then there were the thousands who relied on Llanwern steel, like the corner shops, housing, schools, who all benefited. They built Caldicot and Ringland for the works. Lots of places were built for the steelworks. The pubs, you couldn't get in the Waterloo in Nash on Saturdays, you couldn't even get close to it. Full of Irishmen, it was, the navvies. In the fifties and sixties, it was always the Paddy that built everything, and they were bloody brilliant workers. They built two massive camps round here, one on the army camp, I think about a thousand, and then they built a big caravan site. And all those people used to jump on my school bus when we went to school. It was a 32-seater and there was about 80 by the time they finished.'

Steelmaking had ceased at the site by 2021 with the loss of 1,300 jobs. The effect startled those living under the shadow of the works. Mike George and his neighbours suddenly became aware of life around them again: 'I mean, you would never think that in my short lifetime, I would see it go up, and then see it blown down. There was always background noise, you just got used to it. But when they stopped, I realised I could hear the traffic in Tennyson Avenue again, and hear birds again, and airplanes flying overhead. It had all been blocked out by the background noise of the steelworks.'

The new order led to refreshed efforts to conserve the dwindling wildlife. The Cardiff Bay barrage scheme in 2000, led to the establishment of the Newport Wetlands reserve, to mitigate losses of wildlife habitat at Nash. A purpose-built visitor and education centre for the site was opened in 2008 by the Royal Society for the Protection of Birds (RSPB) covering an area of over 438 hectares from Uskmouth to Goldcliff. Its reedbeds, saline lagoons, wet grassland and scrub attracted a wealth of wetland birds. During the 2000s, Angela Horup was, for a time, the only horse-mounted warden in Wales when she volunteered here. Her father was bought up on a farm behind Nash church. The sea held her in thrall: 'As a child, the sea was an object of fascination. We spent most of our time at the sea wall. We used to walk right out into the mud at low tide, which must have caused a lot of worries for the grown-ups.' On one occasion someone came out to rescue her: 'I can remember quite vividly, I was with my mother and her friend, and this poor lady had to struggle out after us in all the mud. She was frantic, but we didn't see any danger.'

This coastline became an increasingly busy thoroughfare, with vessels arriving from all over the world, as Newport Docks grew in importance. But there are hazards here, and many ships have got into trouble on the invisible and shifting sandbanks. The dangers were not always confined to geography alone.

The pills (a Welsh word for a tidal creek) on this lonely coast were used by people, sometimes locals, and even men of the cloth, to ransack wrecked ships. The head of the priory at Goldcliff, Philip de Gopillarius, was accused of stealing from wrecks in 1334. According to Roy Palmer in his *Folklore of Old Monmouthshire* (1998, Logaston): '... Philip de Gopillarius, and a monk, some clergymen, and 50 other persons from Newport, Nash and Goldcliff, Clevedon and Portishead, were charged with taking wine, and other goods from a vessel wrecked off Goldcliff. A hole in the sea wall, was thought to be the entrance to a tunnel leading to the priory.'

The Severn Sea demanded much of its sailors. In August 1902, a Newport pleasure steamer, the Heather Bell, became stranded off Nash on its return journey from Bristol, with over 200 passengers. One newspaper reported that '... at 11pm she ran onto the East Usk Patch, and remained fast on the mud. Some of the passengers were landed at Nash by the tugs that went to assist the vessel. It is understood the vessel's skipper is new to her, and to the port. Apparently the East Usk light at Goldcliff, was mistaken for the Lighthouse on the St Brides' side, and the vessel ran her bows into the mud bank, instead of getting down the channel, as far as Bell Buoy before turning into the Usk channel.'

In the wrong conditions, drama can quickly turn into

tragedy, as happened to the crew of another stricken ship in January 1901: 'Clean swept by the seas. Feared loss of all hands. A large vessel has been wrecked off Goldcliff, in addition to the Norwegian barque also reported. She has been practically clean swept, only a portion of the hull and rigging being visible on Saturday morning. No news of the safety of the crew can be learned, and it is feared that they have perished.' *Star of Gwent*, January 4th, 1901.

The East Usk Lighthouse in Nash has served its time well, warning sailors on many a storm-whipped night. It was built in 1893, and tended by the same local family for generations. Originally built on legs, it was incorporated into the sea wall when the sea defences were improved. It was lit by twelve gas cylinders, and was finally converted to electricity in 1972. The chronicler Fred Hando spoke to Mr Herbert Stevens of Manor Farm, Whitson, in the 1950s, a man who had witnessed a shipwreck within sight of the shore at East Usk Lighthouse, in the early part of the 20th century. The community pulled together to save or salvage those lost to the storm. Mr Stevens: 'We collected the men living nearby, and made our way to the Lighthouse. The tide was going out, and soon we were able to reach the wreck. One drowned sailor lay on the mudbank, the other four – they were the crew of a Bristol trader laden with general cargo – were lashed to the mast, all dead. We carried them, and laid them on the floor of the bellringers' room in Nash church tower.' (*Hando's Gwent*, ed Chris Barber 1989, Blorenge Books).

St Mary's in Nash, was regularly used as a makeshift mortuary for sea drownings, and for those who lost their lives in the reens too. Hando met with Cornelius Cox, who was the churchwarden for much of his life. If the victims were not known to local families, they were brought up, and laid on the tower floor by Mr Cox. He was called upon the evening the Bristol trader was lost. He offered his account of the events to Hando: 'I remember it alright,' he said. 'It was my job to ring the bell for evening service, and that evening I did it standing among five corpses! I still think that they might have done for once without the bell.'

Many people, both well- and little-known, have enjoyed the quiet beauty of the Levels over the years. One of its more recent advocates, is the Welsh naturalist Iolo Williams, who described the Levels as 'gloriously beautiful, rich in biodiversity, and utterly irreplaceable'. One of its visitors was the daughter of the Second World War prime minister, Winston Churchill. Margaret Gutteridge explained: 'Every Christmas during the war, we were picked up in an army lorry, and all us children were taken to the Pye Corner camp for a Christmas party. We had great fun, and they really looked after us.' There was another camp near the Uskmouth Power Station, home to women soldiers as well as men. 'They used to travel around on their push bikes,' recalls Margaret. 'There was one woman soldier, who used to stop and talk to me because I had a pet lamb. It was only many months later that I discovered she was Winston Churchill's daughter.'

All three of Churchill's daughters, Diana, Sarah and Mary, served with the forces, but Mary seems the most likely candidate since she was with the Auxiliary Territorial Service (ATS), working on mixed anti-aircraft (AA) batteries. According to Neville Waters, AA guns were in place at Pye Corner. 'When I was in school, the army requisitioned all the land down where the power station is, for a big camp, right opposite Newport Docks and at Pye Corner.' The military, and its weaponry surrounded their farm: 'At our next-door farm, a couple of fields away, there was a search light unit, and anti-aircraft guns.'

The AA guns were there to protect Newport docks. The RAF was there as well, and so was Glyn Vincent, whose family farm stood opposite the entrance to Newport docks on the other side of the river. The family normally hid inside the farmhouse when an enemy raid started: 'We would get underneath the stairs when bombs were going off.' On this occasion, however, he witnessed an aerial pursuit: 'The one night, I'll always remember, is when we saw two Spitfires chasing a German bomber that was dropping bombs, [in order to] to get a bit more speed up. One [bomb] went off just by Nash Road, and another by Pye Corner. My father turned round, and said, "the next one is our [house]." But it wasn't. The bomb fell in the field opposite.' Relieved, and safe, the family turned in for the night. It wasn't the end of the story: 'The next morning the bomb went off, and blew the ceilings down, and everything else in the house.'

Chapter 7

Old boats, cannon balls, and pre-historic footprints – Nash to Newport

With so many attacks on Newport, it was inevitable there would be casualties. Margaret Gutteridge had witnessed one near Goldcliff, when an enemy aircraft was caught in the searchlights. 'We saw it shot down and crash into the River Severn. The next day a few of us children found out a German pilot had been washed up on the beach, so we decided to go and see him.' She and her pals did not get very far: 'The local policeman sent us home, and told us he would speak to our fathers if we came back.'

Neville Waters recalled meeting some of the defenders, although he was more impressed by their catering than their military ware: 'My uncle lived on a nearby farm, and my father would take me up there to see him. One day I wandered up to where the soldiers were, and they were about to have breakfast. The cook was there out in the field, leaning over a fire made up of a few bricks, and an iron grid, with a frying pan on top, and they were frying eggs for all these chaps. I've never seen such a big frying pan, it was about 18-inches in diameter, with 30 eggs in it being fried.'

The weather brightens as I approach the Mendalgief Levels. As I near Newport, the rural surroundings give way to a more urban and industrialised scene. I've arranged to meet someone at the museum for a deep-dive into The Levels' ancient history. But first I stop and grab a coffee. It's a chance to reflect on everything I've seen and heard so far. I'm reminded of something Martin Morgan told me back at Black Rock. Lave net fishermen have become highly attuned to the potential of seemingly featureless items in the mud. They have joined the band of amateur sleuths in their discovery of dozens of ancient fishing baskets, intact and preserved, out in the estuary mud.

He and his fellow fishermen were in the news in 2020, when they found the enormous, elongated horns of an auroch, an extinct cattle species that could stand nearly six feet tall. On other days you might find a Victorian ink bottle or china plates: 'When we were kids we would go out, and find baskets occasionally. They would be uncovered one day, and then covered the next. But after the second Severn Bridge was built, certain areas out there started to scour away. They were constantly changing; you'd have pools where there were never pools before, banks where there were never banks before.'

The potential for new discoveries increased after a storm in 2006. Martin and his fellow fishermen stumbled across dozens of baskets, and some big putchers too. 'We'd never seen so many, so we phoned Rick Turner at Cadw. Rick came down, and had a look, and then Reading University got involved as well. On the day we took the archaeologists down it was a terrible, terrible January day, howling a gale.' But there was excitement when Martin showed them what they had found. 'There were lots of these urn-shaped baskets, and many others too, all completely different. You would be looking at them, and they looked like they were made yesterday. It was amazing.' The baskets were later carbon-dated to between the 11th and 15th centuries.

For Martin, his discoveries felt like a deep connection to the past. 'When we are fishing out there, it feels like we are treading in the footsteps of our ancestors, our forefathers, and to me, that's a big part of it. Discovering these ancient baskets shows that people have been fishing out there forever. I feel it's a gift really.'

The Roman docks at Caerleon, a Bronze Age boat, and 15th-century clinker-built merchant vessel, are just three examples of the maritime heritage of this seagoing city. The discoveries have led to calls for a dedicated site to exhibit these finds. Meanwhile, the 15th-century merchant ship, found in 2002 during the construction of the Riverfront Theatre and Arts Centre, is temporarily housed in a temperature-controlled warehouse outside Newport, and is undergoing lengthy conservation. The ship was, says Bob Trett, former curator of Newport Museum & Art Gallery, the jewel in the crown, and 'the biggest individual item I've ever dealt with.'

There have been many archaeological finds on the Levels. Each time the Severn tide pulls away, another world is revealed, releasing relics from the past: clay pipes, cannon balls, ship's crockery, footprints, trackways, ink bottles, fish baskets, ships, boats, and much more. These are rich hunting grounds for amateur and professional sleuths. But when the tide returns, the muddy secrets are hidden once more, making this the most challenging of places to excavate, salvage and record. Nonetheless, the potential for outstanding discoveries here is real.

Mike Mazzoleni reached for an old biscuit tin as we chatted. It was filled with the spoils of his mud-larking forays on the Severn foreshore, and included clay pipes, bits of them at least. Mike has stumbled upon other items too, including at least one dangerous discovery: 'I found a cannonball down there once, and it was my pride and joy. It was covered in barnacles, and I used a hammer to knock the them off, and then I said to myself, "What's that indentation there?" And thought nothing of it. Eventually, I took it to Newport Museum, and someone there said, "Whatever you do don't hit this with anything, because that's the detonation point!"'

The Severn mud is thick, oozing, viscous – it gets every-where, and it's hard to negotiate: 'There are certain places on the shoreline that I know like the back of my hand, and I know where to get the good stuff, but you have to go through a pain barrier,' said Mike. He even designed his own mud-larking uniform: 'You lose your wellies about ten times when you're out there. Instead, just go out with the oldest pair of slippers you've got, and a pair of shorts, and don't expect to come back with anything on, because it is absolutely brutal out there.'

One of the most enthusiastic archaeologists of the Levels, was the late Rick Turner OBE (1952-2018). His knowledge and passion for its history, were the inspiration for the Living Levels project. He pioneered the study of fish baskets pre-served in the estuary mud, and other finds. When the second Severn crossing was being constructed, it revealed a whole crop of artefacts. He had a particular interest in wetland areas, especially the Gwent Levels, and saw the value of them, not just archaeologically, but environmentally too, and worked to protect them. In his work with Cadw in the early 1990s, he recognised that the Levels were vulnerable to development. This fear was heightened by the proposed diversion of the M4, which represented an even greater threat to the area.

Another figure prominent in efforts to preserve the heritage of the Levels was Derek Upton (1941-2005), who made his mark in the difficult conditions of the tidal area. Navigating a safe route out onto the estuary mud is a challenge, as Mike Mazzoleni discovered. He managed with an apparent inbuilt compass of this treacherous coastal area. Derek worked at the steelworks, and had no formal training in archaeology, but his extraordinary discoveries led to him becoming known on the Levels as Mr Severn Estuary. He ventured out to areas at low tide where others dared not go, and came across some amazing archaeological objects that stunned locals and academics alike. His contribution was acknowledged by leading academics, including the 'mud professor', Professor Martin Bell of Archaeological Science at the University of Reading, a voice among many who credited Derek with alerting the authorities, local communities and academics to the rich prehistoric archaeology of the Severn Estuary.

Among Derek's discoveries were a set of Mesolithic human footprints at Magor and Uskmouth, and Bronze Age sites at Caldicot and Redwick. His work led to the establishment of the Severn Estuary Research Committee, and a national recognition of the importance of the Levels and coastal archaeology.

Derek Upton was an inspirational figure to many, including Martin Bell the 'mud prof'. Martin spoke of their first encounter, at a conference to consider the environmental impact of the Severn Barrage. 'The conference was really designed to try and alert people to the archaeology of the estuary. He got me interested in the things that he had found on the Welsh side. I think his greatest contribution was knowing the estuary so intimately. He wandered around there from childhood. That was his leisure time activity going out there, looking at the birds and the wildlife, and finding archaeological items.'

Shifting sands, and treacherous tides... it takes a particular knowledge to navigate the coastline here and Derek was generous in sharing what he knew with others. Martin: 'Derek taught me a lot. He'd walked the estuary, and had a sort of map in his mind. Because the mud and the sand are moving around all the time. You can go down there, find something, and go back two weeks later, and it's gone, covered up again for the next four years. But he would be able to take you to a spot where he had found something years before: he knew exactly where it was. It was an astonishing ability.'

In 1985, Derek generated much excitement when he discovered an Iron Age trackway. Radiocarbon dating placed it at between 2,370 – 2,770 years old.

Bob Trett also came to know Derek well. 'When I first arrived at the museum here in Newport, we reckoned there were about 14 items in the collections from the pre-history of Gwent, not just Newport.' Yet Trett had thirteen cases to fill. 'We were very short on material. So, we started to cultivate a lot of metal detectorists, and I became involved with the Glamorgan Gwent Archaeology Trust, who were a great help.'

Derek's discoveries stunned everyone. 'He came in with a load of Iron Age pottery once, which had my eyeballs going out on stalks,' said Trett. 'He told me that when he was a child in Sudbrook, he used to wander over the sea wall, and walk out to the mud flats.

'He would point out things, so I went down and had a little investigation in a channel, where all the Iron Age pottery was coming out, and two colleagues walked out on the fore-shore. They finished up at a place called Chapel Tump, which is a couple of miles away, and they came running back saying, "we've got a prehistoric platform." It was out in the estuary. So, I went and had a look and some hurdles had been laid down, and were pegged into the ground. Of course, we had no idea of a date, but we managed to get a whole series of radiocarbon dating, and it turned out to be Iron Age.'

Derek was to make yet more extraordinary discoveries. 'Alongside this, we started finding Bronze Age pottery, and then we found a Bronze Age working site,' said Bob, 'where bits of flint were uncovered, and pits in which they had been burning. From then on the discoveries just snowballed. At Magor Pill, he found all sorts of things out there, from all different periods. And then we went to Goldcliff and started finding Mesolithic, and some early prehistoric material.' As the team went further out from Goldcliff, they discovered woven fish traps. 'And then we suddenly found a hut. It was just the base of the hut, but it had partitions inside it, and it had a reed floor, and that turned out to be Iron Age and part of a small settlement.'

The discovery of ancient footprints was the pinnacle: 'Derek rang up very excitedly one day, and said he'd just been to Nash, near the mouth of the Usk, and had found a set of human footprints. It was amazing.'

In the 1990s, intertidal archaeology was a new and emerging science, and at the forefront was Professor Martin Bell. I meet up with the mud professor on the sea wall. The tide is up, and we won't be venturing out there today. It feels like I've missed an opportunity. To Martin, it remains as ripe for exploration, as it was when he was first alerted to this area: 'I'm an environmental archaeologist. I'm interested in people's relationship with the landscape, and how people have changed the landscape, using evidence from sediments, vegetation, and animals. And that's, in a way, why I'm so passionate about the Living Levels, because it helps to bring together the archaeology.'

He has spent much of his professional life studying the shifting sands of the Severn Estuary. He shares his boyish enthusiasm for discovering the story behind every find, from clay pipe to animal bone, to fragments of Second World War aircraft. He has mud appeal, and enthusiasts flock to his public lectures.

The archaeological potential of the Severn Estuary was late arriving. Martin: 'Archaeologists were a bit fixated on dry land sites, and in South Wales, I think, very fixated on Roman and medieval archaeology. The prehistory of the estuary (and most of these sediments are prehistoric) had been little worked on. Even now, we know far more about the pre-history of the wetland in the intertidal zone than we do about the dry land. Which is extraordinary.

'The sediments are wet all the time, and this preserves wood structures, and a lot of environmental evidence. And things like footprints, not just human footprints, but animal footprints. With most dry land situations, all the wooden posts, and things that make up trackways or buildings, have decayed away. In a wetland context, you find the wood preserved. You never quite know what you are going to find, and it's very exciting.'

In 1957, with increased production in major industries such as steel, coal and motor cars leading to a rise in wages, export earnings and investment, Prime Minister Harold Macmillan was compelled to comment to fellow Conservatives that 'most of our people have never had it so good'. He was painting a rosy picture. Although the 1950s was a time of full employment, and more people than ever bought their own home and ran a car, the UK manufacturing base, stronger than ever, represented a real threat to the farmland of the Levels.

The change had started far earlier. Many areas had been built over, like the wet, marshy land on the edges of Newport. Newport used to be a relatively small town. In the medieval period, it had a castle to defend the river crossing, a market, a mill, a few houses, and a wharf. However by the early 19th century, Newport and South Wales had become the world's biggest producer of iron; a century later, a third of the world's coal was mined nearby. By 1851, Wales was the world's first industrial society; this meant more people were employed by industry than by agriculture. By 1913, 232,000 people worked in 620 mines; by 1920, the figure had risen to over 271,000.

Chapter 8

Cuckoo cheese, vaulting reens, and horse work – St Brides to Marshfield

Leave Newport and take the B road to St Brides, and you pass from the Level of Mendalgief (Mendelgyf) to the Wentloog (Gwynllŵg) Level. Mendalgief, a medieval Welsh kingdom according to the online encyclopaedia Wikipedia, forms part of the threatened green belt separating Newport and Cardiff. At St Brides I take a look around the graveyard. My guilty admission is I love them. The names, hidden stories, triumphs, tragedies, or just quiet heroism. I'm lucky to find the warden there, and I have a tour up the bell tower where names are scratched into the stonework. Looking out, I shudder to think of the 1609 tsunami rolling in here.

None of this was in the mind of Jesse Higgins, when he arrived at St Brides in the 1900s. He had left hilly Herefordshire, tempted by the rich farmland of the Levels at St Brides. He arrived on his horse and cart, lock, stock, and barrel, in search of work. I chatted to his grandson Robert, who was born in 1949, and still lives next door to his birthplace in St Brides. He shows me the old milking parlour and stables, and what remains of their orchard. The biggest change, he said is the road outside. It's a rat run, he says, a cut through to Cardiff and it's awful. After Jesse Higgins settled in, he steadily built up a modest dairy herd, and eventually a milk round: 'I think there was perhaps half a dozen cows,' said Robert. 'When my father was a boy, he used to help. Sometimes the horse wouldn't come, when they were preparing to go out delivering milk, so they sent the dog to get it in. The dog would jump on the horse's back and the horse would stand still, so grandfather could catch the horse, put it on the cart, and then go and deliver the milk from churns in the back of the cart.'

Another farmer who kept cows was Glynn Vincent. He told me how his parents, Fred and Ethel, also kept a few cows on their tenanted farm, rented from the Tredegar Estate, at Nash. Glynn was expected to milk five cows, by hand, before school: 'I can always remember the old man saying, "you're lying in bed and the sun is shining through the window. Get up!" It would take me about half an hour to milk five cows, and they used to bottle the milk up and sell it.

'Dad had a horse and cart, and they poured the milk into a big round bucket with a lid on it, and then they would pour it out with a half-pint ladle. And you'd fill the customer's jug up to the rim. If you spilled a little bit, they would say, "I'm not having that," and I'd have to go back and put a bit more in.'

The large number of dairy farms on the Levels meant cheese-making was once common here, and the Levels became rather well-known for it too. The mining communities of South Wales were hungry for farmhouse cheese, and provided a healthy market for the Levels' cheese makers. Thomas Jones of Marshfield was one.

Marshfield lies on the other side of the Newport to Cardiff railway tracks. In the early part of the 20th century, Mr Jones travelled to Caerphilly Cheese Fair to sell his cheese to coal miners because, he rationalized, 'mine owners did not like to take meat underground'. However, in 1837 Mr W. Phillips of Whitson considered cheese from 'the lowlands of Caldicot and Wentloog to be capable of great improvement.' As an incentive to encourage exemplary cheese making, he offered a prize, to female competitors only, of a silver teapot to the value of ten guineas, for the best sample of cheese made from a dairy of not less than 12 cows.

At Peterstone, I'm greeted by Arthur Thomas who started milking cows on his father's farm when he was 13. Arthur's accent has a gentle lilt to it. I feel soothed by his voice. His father made the curiously named cheese: 'When the cuckoo comes in April the grass grows more, you end up having a glut of milk. I remember Dad making cheese in the dairy. He'd built the dairy in 1937/38, a wooden structure with all clean lines inside to meet the requirements. We didn't sell the cheese, we just made enough for ourselves from our surplus milk. Our cuckoo cheese tasted a bit like a Caerphilly cheese. Very good it was.'

Reen vaulting was the practical solution to crossing these flat-lands, with hundreds of water channels of varying width, breadth and depth. It required a wooden pout or powt (traditionally a pole used by fishermen to spear salmon) forced into the banks of ditches and reens: imagine a country version of the pole vault. A similar version has even become a spectator sport in another flat landscape, the Netherlands. It is something children did here, in the same way that children elsewhere climbed gates. 'We went vaulting over the grips in the fields to see who could do the widest one,' recalled Val Southall in Marshfield. Val and her childhood friends at Marshfield spent their daylight hours out in the fields on the Levels, armed with their version of a powt, usually a broomstick handle. Glen Vincent, a former Usk Power Station security worker, also used a broomstick when he went exploring the Levels from his Nash home: 'If you went out, you couldn't walk across the reens, so you used a pole. Used to fall in a few times, that was normal.'

Fred Hando preferred balancing on fallen trees to vaulting to cross reens. He was a Newport schoolteacher, who chronicled the history of Gwent in a series of newspaper articles and books between the 1920s and 1960s: 'Father's passion for eel-pie took him and us to the Great Reen, and while he fished, we enjoyed the thrill of emulating Blondin, [Charles Blondin, best known for crossing the Niagara Falls on a tightrope], crossing and re-crossing the narrow tree trunks which spanned the reen. Yet we never mustered sufficient courage to pole-vault the reens, as the farm labourers did with their powts.' *Hando's Gwent,* (ed Chris Barber 1989, Blorenge Books).

Much as a child brought up in a hilly area becomes familiar with peaks and troughs, so children brought up in a flat, watery landscape also adapt. I was brought up on the banks of the Severn, and my parents put the fear of god in us if we ever went near the river. Sue Waters: 'If you grow up with reens around you, you are always aware of them. I think if we had visitors or other children come to play, we'd always tell them, "don't go near the reens". I think up until five or six-years-of-age, you could then be trusted to play outside, but you always had somebody with you.'

However, says Sue, 'in the church registers every year, you'd read of somebody having drowned, a child or an adult, or they had fallen in accidentally, and couldn't get out. You know, if you get your feet in the muck, it almost drags you under.' Kath Johnson was also warned by her parents to 'never play near a reen, because if you fall in you might not get back out. Some of the reens have a peat base, they're not all clay; well, peat will suck you down.'

The craft of managing the reens was handed down from generation to generation. When I reach St Brides, I meet Gordon Shears. He has farmed the land here all his life, and is another Leveller who hasn't strayed far. He sits in an armchair, overlooking the road. He is retired now and all his animals are gone. There's a wistful atmosphere here, his wife Linda especially misses the livestock. Gordon is quiet and reserved. It is his wife who is the chatty one. When he speaks, I have to lean forward to catch what he is saying.

His family managed the reens on their farm, when they moved to St Brides in 1934. Gordon's father, William, originally farmed in Michaelston-y-Fedw. In 1916 he was called up, aged 18, and sent to the trenches in France, where he was put in charge of a mule train taking supplies to the front. Struggling through mud, dampness, and misery, he would end up suffering from asthma for the rest of his life. Many of the farm's responsibilities fell on Gordon's shoulders: 'If my father's chest was bad, he'd sit by the fire for perhaps two days, because he couldn't get his breath.' Tractor power was still in the future for many farmers in the 1930s and 1940s. 'We had cart horses which helped a lot at haymaking time. They were [named] Flower, Blossom, Diamond and Bonnie. I used to drive them in the field, raking or tedding. Flower was on the tedder. She'd plod up the field away from the gate, but she'd walk twice as fast back, because she thought she was on her way home. Then you'd have a job to turn her around to get her to go back again. We had what we called a pike, like a crane, for digging in the hay, and the horse would haul it on a rope, and it would swing over the rick and pop it on top. But she was willing until the tractor came in 1946, and the tractor used to do the job then.'

Gordon also learned the craft of rick thatching with reed. As he explained to me: 'I used to thatch the ricks with reeds cut from the reens. It was too much for father, so I eventually started doing it. I learned just by watching him. We cut the reeds from the same spot every year, because the reed was nice and fine then. If you got the thick reed, they didn't keep the water off the same.

'I had a very long ladder, and used to lean it against the rick, and wind the twine on a peg, bring the peg over and put a bare peg in, and then wind the string around it.'

The raw material for the pegs was sourced from the local willows: 'I used to cut the pegs from the withy trees, and sharpen them. I've still got a little scar on my leg, where I gashed my trousers and my leg, cutting the pegs one time.

Gordon took great care with his work: 'You'd have four or five rows of strings, and you'd use hand shears to cut along the bottom to make it look tidy [around] the edge, like a half moon piece.'

Farm workers took pride in their handiwork. Ron Perry remembered his father teaching him too: 'The hay ricks were all around the farm, one in each field. We used to like our ricks to look nice and tidy on the outside. At night time, we'd be making thatching pegs with a knife in the kitchen, in front of the fire. Father would cut withy sticks into two-foot, and two-foot six-inch lengths.

'Father was a wonderful thatcher, and he taught me well too. I made my first rick in this field opposite here on Perry Lane in Nash. I used to stand back and look at it, and admire the thatching. A lot of pride if you've done it well.'

But not everyone had the knack. Ron knew someone who struggled: 'We had one old gentleman down here, and he'd go down the field and he'd thatch too; he'd be up there an hour. The first bit of wind and it would be off. He couldn't thatch.'

When I was back at Porton on the Caldicott Level, I visited John Smalls to see one of the oldest thatched cottages on the Levels. It's used as storage today, and the roof is covered with tin sheets, yet inside an old bedstead still stands, and pictures hang on the wall. While there, he shows me the remains of an old orchard. The small farmsteads that characterised this part of the Levels, which relied on orchards like these, depended on a mixed economy, and a degree of self-sufficiency. Robert Higgins' mother would preserve their fruit using a canning machine, hired out by St Brides' Women's Institute. 'We would pick all the pears and the apples from the orchard, and she used to do all the canning.

She would sterilize the cans, put all the fruit in and seal it up, and they were then put on the shelf ready for the winter.' The canner didn't have very far to travel to its next host, Gordon Shears' mother. It was a very busy time and the arrival of the canning machine, heralded three or four days of intensive activity: 'She used to do it here in the kitchen, fixing it to the table, and a couple of people in the village used to come, and help and peel all the fruit. And they could have some of the fruit for helping.' During wartime food rationing, the canning machine became even more popular in the St Brides and Peterstone areas.

Wartime brought other problems to the community. When I met Marjorie Neal at her home in Rumney, she recalled an evening of drama for her mother, about to go into labour with Marjorie's sister, during a bombing raid. 'As a child I was put under a steel table, and I can still remember my father stood outside the front door watching aircraft go over. The searchlight from the field was pointing in the direction of the planes, and the guns at Mardy Farm were trying to hit them.' The last bomb of the war to fall on Cardiff was dropped on the evening Marjorie's sister was born.

'I was staying with my grandmother and aunt in Wentloog Road, and my cousin and I were put under the staircase, which was right by the back door, by the coal shed. My father came up the path on [his] horse to tell us mother had gone into labour. My aunt got on her bike to go to my mother, while my father went up to get the midwife on his horse. We stayed with my grandmother. As my aunt was coming over the railway bridge, which we called the Skew Bridge, a bomb dropped in the field to the right of her. Luckily it didn't explode, though it killed a tree. That dead tree remained there for about 30 years.'

Back in Kath Johnson's farmhouse kitchen at Goldcliff, we talked, sitting by the same table she had used as a bomb shelter, as she recalled the Newport blitz. Some bombs landed off target, a bit too close for comfort: 'Bombs dropped on the shed here, on the end of the house,' said Kath, 'and blew all the windows in.' It was a similar story for Val Southall, at the other end of the Levels at Marshfield. She shudders as she recalls the bombing, close to the family farm at Gelli-ber:

'We were washing up one night, and all of a sudden you could hear this whizzing noise. The German bombers came right over the house, and bombs were dropping all around the farm. It was terrible. There were searchlights over on Penland, one down at Peterstone/St Brides direction, and the sirens were going. The bombing blew the blinds off the windows.'

Another night and another attack: 'The Germans dropped a string of bombs on the reen coming along Marshfield Road, blowing big holes out of it,' said Val. 'The next day there was fish all along the road, and sheep up the trees.' The raiders pinpointed their targets with incendiary bombs: 'The incendiaries would all light up, like fairy land. Afterwards, my brother would go out hunting for shrapnel, and he once found an incendiary bomb that had not gone off. He was walking around with it, and my father shouted, "Get that the hell out of here!"'

The bomb craters formed excellent watering holes for inquisitive children after the war, though most have long since been covered up by Newport's expansion. Arthur Thomas of Peterstone remembers one: 'There was a bomb dropped just behind Green Meadow, and then there was another one in Caer Cor wood, which is just behind Tesco's. That was a good place to go tadpoling when we were kids.'

Back at his family's farm, Gordon Shears had an encounter with an enemy pilot. 'I was in the yard with my father doing something, and looked up and saw a plane and the pilot was waving. He was low down, taking film and photographs of the docks, I suppose. The plane had swastikas on the side. We could even see the face of the pilot.'

Gordon remembers an unexploded bomb, but his neighbours remained blissfully unaware. 'A bomb came down at Ty Coch Farm, and when the army came out in the morning, they said it was an unexploded bomb, with a parachute on it. Two mines had been dropped, one in the field over the road that took the roof off the house, and this one. The people in that house had stayed in there all night, with an unexploded bomb outside. Clueless they were. When the army did eventually detonate it, it left a huge crater, which was there for years.'

Another bomb crater that survived for decades, was near the near railway hub at Rogiet, and Iris Theobald remembers the damage it created: 'It dropped at the top of the Minnet Lane. That was a dud, but it left a huge crater. It was there for years and years. Everyone would go up and look at it. Of course, the bombers were aiming for the Severn Tunnel. Everything was going through the tunnel, the ammunition, everything. It was a big target. But you didn't really think about that.'

Air raids became so frequent that some people ignored them. Iris' dad, a locomotive driver, was one who saw no reason to interrupt his slumbers: 'We were at home when the planes came over once, and a bomb dropped at Rogiet Pool. Dad must have been working nights, so we went upstairs to his bedroom and said, "Dad get up! They're dropping bombs." But he didn't move, just stayed in bed. Didn't seem bothered.' Although Iris' dad survived, others were not so lucky: 'There was another time when a boy was killed near the Rogiet Hotel. He had come out to watch what was going on and was killed. That was sad.'

On some occasions, the enemy aircraft bombed their own people, German and Italian POWs in local camps who were sent to work on farms down here. Val Southall of Marshfield, met some marvellous and memorable POWs at her family farm, Gelli-ber.

'There was a camp up near Castleton, just by the Coach and Horses. It's a nursing home now. I must have been 14 or 15, and they sent this Italian bloke down to our farm, but he couldn't speak English, and my uncle used to tell me to tell him what to do. Well, I used to get into a state.'

Sometime later, the farm took on a German POW whose skill as a tailor came in handy. 'We had a barrage balloon that was made of white silk that had come down in a field,' said Val. 'So my brother went out and dragged this blinking parachute in, and we had it in the house for ages. Then we learned that this German POW was a tailor before the war.' When Val's mother showed him the parachute, he offered to make her something. 'He made a blouse out of the silk, and I wore that to death, because you couldn't get clothes during the war. And my brother, who worked on the docks, found two rolls of grey, serge-like material, and the German offered to make a suit out of that as well. They'd bring him down and fetch him back, and he made mother a jacket and two skirts out of the serge, and she wore them for years.'

Another of their POWs was more formal: 'We had one German POW, tall fella with blonde hair. When aunt was cooking breakfast, he had these boots, and when he came in, he'd click his heels together and say, "Good morning, Mrs Parsons, how are you today? You look very nice in that dress." He even used to play our piano.'

Some POWs took to farming life, others didn't. At St Brides, Gordon Shears' father had Italian POWs helping on the farm: 'One was a tall thin fella. His name was Gatti, and he was a hard worker. He told us he had been drafted into the Italian army, and wasn't happy about it. I think he was glad to be captured. Then there was the other one, who was the exact opposite of him. He was short and dumpy, and he was a lazy so and so.'

The former POW Alessandro Mazzoleni proved to be a hard worker too. His son Mike told me how he started milking about 20 cows, 'seven days a week at Court Farm. And that's when he met my mother, at a dance down in the Farmer's Arms at Goldcliff. These Italians were handsome guys, very handsome, compared to a big, fat, old, grumpy farmer! And that's why I'm here today.'

Robert Higgins' parents, also in St Brides, were air raid wardens and saw some unusual sights: 'Coming back from Newport one time, my mother got stopped by the police. "You can't go any further, we've got an unexploded bomb," they told her. So knowing the Moors very well, she decided to go home another way. She avoided the police cordon by taking a cross-country route via footbridges and fields, cutting around the road that had been blocked. But then she came across the bloke who was trying to dig the bomb out and he said, "Come on over and have a quick look!" And she looked at the bomb, and then just continued her way home.

'When they used to drop parachutes, and incendiary bombs to light up everything, my grandfather used to go out with a bucket of water to put them out, and to get his hands on the silk parachutes. Anything they could use they would use during the war.'

The antics of the TV series Dad's Army was, for many of the post-war generation, their only introduction to the Home Guard. It was an affectionate portrayal, but there was truth in some of their bumbling actions. Gordon Shears: 'I remember the Home Guard down here at St Brides. They had a pillbox on the ground down past the lakes, and they were supposed to be watching the Bristol Channel. Well, the commander turned up there one night and found them all asleep. There was a riot.'

The Home Guard was not taking forty winks, when Stephanie Davies' father was strolling near the sea wall at Rumney, early in the war: 'We would often see them parading along the sea wall. My father was walking over there one evening, and one of them appeared in front of him, in uniform, holding a gun, shouting, "Halt! Who goes there!" It gave him the fright of his life.'

Sisters and brother Ruth, Mary and Doug Richardson, now all in their nineties, have fond memories of their childhood in Marshfield before the war years. They have been part of the Marshfield Church congregation all their lives. Until recently, Doug was still a member of the choir (nearly eight decades worth), and Mary played the organ for Sunday services for eighty years. I first met them on a sunny day at the St Brides' church summer fete, and arranged to meet them again in Coedkernew.

As children, they were forbidden from playing in the reens – 'too dangerous' – but picnics on the sea wall were a regular summertime treat. Mary Richardson: 'Mum and dad would pack up a lunch and we'd have to walk down. We had no transport, and it was a good couple of miles. My sister Ruth was on the beach once, and she cut her toe on a piece of glass. And I can see my mother now, carrying Ruth, who was only a tot, in her arms to get to the road, and a baker's van came along and gave her a lift to the doctors. The doctor had a surgery in the vicarage then, and the baker took her there to have her foot dressed. That was the end of our picnic that day.'

The foreshore was part of Robert Higgins' playground too. With his gang of friends, he improvised exploring the Severn Estuary mud, making makeshift mud sledges. They were the ideal vehicles for the muddy area: 'We used to go down the foreshore. It's changed now, but it used to have big open areas with water, and [we] made rafts and explored down there; all the kids in the village used to go out on the mud. We would get bits of wood, some nails, a couple of drums, and we'd tie them all together with rope.'

Young as they were, they realised the dangers: 'You had to be very careful because there are risks out there. But we used to stay on what we called the 'black stuff'. It was like peat. If you stayed on that you'd be all right. If you got off it, you'd drop about two or three feet, and you didn't know how deep the mud was then. And then, when you saw the tide coming in, that's when you'd get back out.'

St Brides church has a plaque in the porch that marks the level of the infamous flood of 1606, as do the churches at Goldcliff and Nash. Gordon Shears' farm, too, is just a field away from the sea wall. Too close to comfort for some, but not for Gordon. He has seen holes in it, including on at least one occasion, a hole so big a vehicle could drive through: 'You go out the back here, and you can hear the sea at night. Now and again, I used to worry, but they've raised the wall a couple of times. Before it was higher up, [the sea] would splash all over, and pour down the dip at the back of it, and I got drenched a couple of times when I was younger.'

Despite the mud and dangerous tides, a dip in the Severn Sea was a rite of passage for some children. The adventurous, including railway worker Terry Theobald, tried it at Rogiet. The Moors were his playground, and so was the Severn Sea. It was for the bold, the brave, or the foolish: 'I'm almost a non-swimmer,' said Terry, 'but some friends of mine were great swimmers, and they'd play water polo, frightening the life out of me because when the tide was high, they used to dive in off the sea wall, and go underneath the filthy water. Then they would swim sideways then disappear. I thought, "Oh my god, they're dead!" Then they'd pop up 60 or 70 yards away. Oh, they were buggers. They were fantastic swimmers, but they were the only ones with enough courage to go in really.' Terry can remember local drownings: 'There's quite a few people who didn't do so well. But none of us lot. There was an inbuilt instinct. We knew about the tides. We knew if you followed the tide out, you had enough time for a few hours messing about, before you had to get back.'

The Severn has the third highest tidal range in the world, only the Bay of Fundy (North America) and Ungava Bay (Hudson Straits) are higher. The tidal range on the Severn can be as much as 15 metres (49 feet). Tides are more regular than clockwork. It comes in and out, twice a day, but timings can vary. Published tide timetables are a must down here. Though it wasn't something youngsters used to think about. Despite his mother's warning, Martin Morgan still used to go swimming out from the dock at Black Rock. 'I learned to swim there. We never had tide tables, but we'd be out there playing, fishing, collecting things, just exploring generally.

'Our childhood, when you think about it, was pretty tough, but we had the estuary to play in. With the last of the flood, we'd be diving off the dock, swim to Black Rock, and they'd go back with the first of the ebb. Several times we've had to swim across gullies in the estuary, exploring, fishing, digging, and collecting tackle. That's where it all started for me really, fishing with a rod and line. We didn't have a fishing rod. You had to make up a hand line. We just collected stuff that people lost off the foreshore.'

There were risks, of course, said Martin. He remembered a few close calls: 'There was a time when we were all swimming in the dock, where the water from the Severn Tunnel pumping station is pumped out. It's quite a good swimming area in there, bit cold with the spring water. It was high tide, and somebody pushed this boy in, and he couldn't swim. They thought it was great fun. So, he was splashing around in the water and suddenly, he shouted, "I can't swim", and he went straight down, he'd gone. The water is pretty deep there, so two or three of the other boys dived in, got hold of him, and they were able to drag him out. It was quite frightening.'

One of the big local attractions was a sea pool at the lighthouse in St Brides. The lighthouse was a popular day trip for visitors from Cardiff and Newport. They arrived on bike or foot, by bus, or charabanc. Some even set up camp on the roadside for this mini getaway. Nothing remains of it today, but the lighthouse Pub is still there, and a café too. In the 1930s, Val Southall visited with her mother: 'We used to walk down there. It was a day's outing really, walking from Peterstone, all along the sea wall. I remember the last time I went there as a child she bought me a toy from one of the booths that used to be down there. There were shops too, some fairground stalls, a carousel. You'd get buses bringing people from Newport for the day. There were shows with entertainment there as well.'

There was no swimming for David Hurn, but the lighthouse was the unlikely location for his return to his Welsh roots. He was a Magnum photographer who enjoyed 1960s swinging London, working on Bond films, and the cult classic, Barbarella. He told me he quit the bright lights in 1970, and arrived at the lighthouse in his camper van. 'Well it was practical,' he told me when we met. 'I had the van when I was in London. My initial plan was to just come back for her for a year. So it seemed to me illogical to buy somewhere. So what I did was park the van basically on the Levels, by the lighthouse there, near Newport, and I joined Newport Rugby Club, and used their shower facilities there. And that's how I lived for the year.'

Chapter 9

Betty the Fish, Finding Nemo and saltmarsh sheep – Marshfield to Peterstone

The journey between Marshfield and Peterstone is short, but it is a busy stretch. The road runs parallel with the footpath, and traffic is constant. The old coast road, which looks out across to Flat Holm Island, isn't very pretty as you approach Cardiff.

The city, not the sea, has encroached here, and robust sea defences have made Rumney residents like Marjorie Neal feel safer. We sit in her farmhouse kitchen, as she talks about farming at the outer edges of Wentlooge Levels: 'In years gone by, on a high tide, you would see, from the bedroom windows, waves crashing against the lynches (the flat grass area further out). Now the sea wall is raised, you don't see that.'

Some of the raw materials for the wall came from unusual sources, according to Marjorie. When the demolition men pulled down the nation's premier rugby stadium, Cardiff Arms Park, a lot of it, she said, ended up in the sea wall. Now, thanks to the great game of rugby, she feels safer.

Whether it's netting salmon at Black Rock, catching eels at Rogiet, spearing flounders at Newport, or leisure fishing at St Brides, fishing had been carried on here since the land was first settled. In the 1950s, a lady known as Betty the Fish, lived in a tiny hovel close to the sea wall at Peterstone. Her diminutive figure was often seen carrying a basket of freshly caught fish balanced on her head. She walked from

St Brides, through to Marshfield and Castleton, and finally on to Cefn Mably, in time for breakfast to sell the fish. There would have been many more like her. For working class families, fresh fish from the sea or reens, was free, abundant, and an essential part of their diet.

Cockles, too, were harvested, not in such abundance as Penclawdd, but enough to provide free food for one sitting. Iris Theobald spoke of her cockling days with her *grancha*, (grandfather), when we met at her home in Rogiet. 'He used to go out into the estuary to a place we called the Bedwins, fishing for cockles. But you've got to be careful because there's like a patch of sand right out in the water, and when the tide comes in, it comes in quickly on one side, and you don't notice it until it is too late. If you're not careful, you could get trapped out there. You had to know the tides.

'Everyone fished. It was good food in those days. I used to help *grancha* make his fishing nets in his little cottage in Caldicot; a lot of local people made their own nets.'

When he went fishing for eels, Iris' nephew, Terry Theobald, learned to treat the Severn with respect: 'There was a bunch of kids and we used to walk down, along on the sea wall, with our bags and spades. Then we'd follow the tide out, right into the middle of the estuary trying to catch the eels. We used to do what we called eel bashing.'

One time Terry was caught out by a fast tide: 'Someone shouted "the tide's coming boys," and off we went trudging through the mud to get in. By the time we got a hundred yards or so back in, it had got to us, and the water was rushing up above my wellies, [but] we managed to get onto this slightly higher mud. It was scary.'

Eels were a popular food with many families. Easy to catch and plentiful in those days. Having suffered a devastating decline, there are very few now, and many of the former prime eel fishing haunts have gone, covered over by the steelworks. Kath Johnson went eel fishing there with her father: 'My father used to like eels. We had bean sticks, and you'd have a bit of wire on it and a hook, stick it in the bank, and then go back at night, to see if you had caught any in the reen. I'd fetch them back. Mam used to skin them, then boil them for him.'

Salmon numbers have dropped, but so too have eels. By some estimates, they have faced a 97% decline. At Goldcliff, I met another walker who remembered the roads here with a writhing mass of elvers in the spring.

Jan Preece also recalled eel fishing. He set up a heritage centre at Pilgwenlli, and I look him up when I reach Newport. We meet at his home, not far from the entrance to Newport Docks. Now I count my blessings I got to see him before he died: he was a raconteur, irreverent, funny, and did fascinating work recording the history of Pill. In the 1980s he interviewed prostitutes, who worked at Newport Docks during the war. "They had children to feed," explained Jan.

'I've gone eel fishing here in the 1980s. Just as it was getting dark was always a good time, and on a full moon too, and afterwards we would come back and fill the kitchen sink with eels. They were a common food here in Pill in those days, [but] I can't remember the last time I saw one.' Eels were an easy catch, but some people, like Jan, knew the best places, and which areas to avoid. Under Newport Bridge was a classic spot. 'You'd go there any day on an incoming tide, and catch at least ten or twelve eels. But we tended not to eat them out of the docks, because eels are bottom feeders. You would cut them open, and they'd be full of crude oil. But eels on the river are ok.'

There was another delicacy locals enjoyed. 'Up to the 1970s, fish curry was popular here too, with whiting. We used to catch [whiting] in the river down there. Used to get tonnes of whiting, on the dockside, by the Transporter Bridge with rod and line.' Curiously, French snails were also freely available here, a tasty and cheap supper for some. Jan used to collect and cook them in garlic butter, French style: 'Snails were a big thing in Pill.' He took me to see an old drystone wall at the bottom of the road. 'This used to be full of French snails bought over originally in the Napoleonic wars.'

The snail secret was shared with local pubs, Jan told me: 'The pubs used to get a massive boiler, and they would boil a couple of sacksful of snails, and just put them on the counter at lunchtime, and have them with garlic butter, and people would just help themselves. The Waterloo pub by the docks was one of them.'

Bev Cawley found her very own Nemo after one of her father's fishing trips: 'Dad and his friend Wyndham used to collect all these fishes in a bucket. While dad and Wyndham were milking, it would be my job to wash these fish in the water tank, because they're covered in mud. And of course, you'd put them in the water tank, and they would come back to life. It would frighten the life out of me. I picked this one up by the tail and he was alive, and floating around the tank for weeks. He had a dorsal fin and it used to come up like a fan, a mottled sort of colour, pinks and greens and blues. I believe it was a gurnard. Great fun for me though.'

I've become so used to seeing the reens here, I've taken them for granted. But do I really understand what they do? I stopped off in a pub in Marshfield, and one regular explained it to me, speaking very slowly, tapping the counter to emphasize each point: I was embarrassed but at least he got his point across. 'Rainfall and run-off from the surrounding upland areas create a naturally wet landscape,' he said. 'To make it habitable for people and livestock, an interconnected system of open ditches takes water off the land and out to sea.

'When you're farming here, you have to know the names

of your reens so that when you're talking to the Drainage Board, or the River Boards as they once were, you can tell them the name of the reen you want cast,' explains Sue Waters. (Casting means clearing the reen to prevent it becoming silted up and overgrown.)

Over the years, Sue Waters created her own cartography of the landscape around her. 'I've mapped most of the area, with the reens marked on them for future generations,' she says. 'I've detailed absolutely everything. Goldcliff, Whitson and parts of Nash. There's a reason why some reens are called what they are: like Monk's Croft, for instance, up just above us, and Windmill Reen – you can imagine where their names come from. Then there is Elver Pill. Elvers are baby eels. A lot of the names are self-explanatory.'

Like most landowners here, Sue understands her farm-land well. 'I know the direction [that] the water flows. So, the Parish Reen goes basically right around the parish of Nash, and we know where the outlets – or gouts – are. These are all things that farmers should know. We know if we need to cast a reen – or clean it out – if the water isn't getting down to a certain part of the farm. As farmers we have to keep an eye on the reens. And every other year, a reen or ditch has to be cast, and we have to bear the cost of it. So, for the mainten-ance, Natural Resources Wales (NRW), pay for a ditcher to clean it out, and after that it's our problem.'

Peterstone's Arthur Thomas describes his childhood home as paradise – 'it was utopia – but has strong views on how the drainage is managed. A former Internal Drainage Board member, he has great respect for the reen network, but worries it has been neglected. There could be consequences: 'These reens are really a necessity on the Moors. I've been a great lover of them all my life. I've always been around them, fallen in them, jumped them, played in them. I mean we had a reen on our farm that ran up hill. But really it was running towards the hill, and went across the road towards Cardiff, and then back down and along. You had to see it to believe it.'

A drainage system going uphill? Defying gravity? It can baffle newcomers. The flow of water is often counter-intuitive, but locals know how it works. A bird's eye view of the Levels, illustrates the scale of drainage here and its necessity, but it can be baffling to outsiders. John Southall: 'Well, with a lot of the reens, the water will flow one direction in the summer, and then in another direction in the winter! But not all of them. It's one of those jobs where you could study as much as you want, and it doesn't help you. You only get to know it by being on the ground, and physically seeing the water moving. These water levels have to be bang on, because it's all perfectly balanced.'

John understands the intricacies of the drainage network. Part of his job and knowledge, is anticipating problems. It would be his Mastermind special subject: 'There's 169 sluices. I know where the issues are likely to occur, because I've seen it so many times, and know which places to check. I can look at a stretch of reen in one location, and I can see how much water is in that reen and I'll be thinking, "Right, it's obviously going to be four miles away in St Brides. Because if it's that low there, it can't be any higher down there."'

Traditionally the farmers would aim to raise the water levels in April, and start to lower them by October. 'It's intricate but it's also logical,' said John. 'It's just that you've got to know the locations of sluices, and you've got to know the amounts of water going down the reens, and how much can be seen going over each sluice. It's just experience really.'

John says his work is all about managing flood risk. 'We don't have responsibility for the main rivers. There are 180 kms of Caldicott & Wentlooge Internal Drainage Board (CWIDB) maintained ditches, and you've got 90 kms of main river, and you've probably got ten times that in private ditches.' John knows the name of every water course – at least those that have a name.

His favourite reen, the Sealand, runs right through St Brides. 'It has beautifully poached banks, and it's the most important in terms of managing flood risk.'

John's work has taken him into the new housing, and commercial developments that have sprung up around existing reens, and have brought added pressures. Some of these areas were farmland as recently as 2000. But if you're new to the area, it's easy to underestimate the importance of a ditch running through your estate.

John points out the drainage that serves the Duffryn Estate near Tredegar Park as an example. 'The reen was there long before that estate was built. The difference is that now the reen is a lot bigger than it used to be, and wider. It's been widened to accommodate the extra water run-off from all these new houses. You've got to remember, all the water that falls on those rooves, goes straight into the ditch. Whereas before it would have fallen on land that would have absorbed it, so you get extra water run-off going into ditches. And we have to manage and accommodate that.

'People don't realise where they are living. I'll say, "Do you realise that your unit here is actually two metres below sea level? Well, there's the sea wall over there, and the tide can get high."

'The only reason this place isn't under water, is because of the work we do maintaining this network of ditches, and reens and ordinary water courses. If it was not for us, you would be under water.

'The most worrying time for me in terms of flood risk is the summer,' says John, 'because the reens are already at high levels. In the winter we prepare for it, so I don't have sleepless nights. In summer you've got reens full of growth, and that reduces the flow rate, you've also got reens kept at a high level, which reduces attenuation. I mean, summer weather events are dicey. The closest we've had to big flooding has always been in the summer. These huge summer storms empty a large amount of water in a very short space of time, on an area that's already full of water. If the ground is particularly dry, it doesn't absorb very well. It just runs off it, straight into the ditch. If the ground is a bit soft, a bit wet, it absorbs it like a sponge. We just have to anticipate and react.'

The sea wall held back the Severn, but the sea brought the benefits of enriched soil, as one Peterstone farmer emphasised. 'Because of the sea wash, this is very, very fertile ground. The ground by the sea wall gets washed once a month with the high tide, and it's great for the soil. Down here it's very, very high in nutrients. We've made bigger fields out of the smaller fields, because it was such a good nutrient land and good grazing.'

He is the third generation of his family to farm on the same spot. 'You can grow good winter wheat down there, four tonne to the acre if you get it right, so long as you are tile-drained or plastic-drained, because it gives us a bit more grazing time.' Wet ground could cause difficulties: 'This ground is not the ground you poach in the winter – you don't graze it hard in the winter. Poach means you have heavy stock, like cattle, that damages the structure of the ground. So, what you do, by about the first week of November, if the weather starts to turn real wet, you get all the heavier stock off, the cattle, horses, and that. But sheep are no problem, they don't hurt the ground as such.' Sheep and their lambs, the farmer told me, got fat on the land: 'No problem at all. It was a pleasure to keep sheep on there, because it's a good bit of ground.

'We used to graze sheep down by what we called the Side Wharf, down Rumney. At certain times of the year, with the high tide, we had to go down and get cattle off there, because the high tide would cover all the grazing ground. So, we would fence, and shut them in 'til the tide had gone back out. But the sheep on the sea wall would get used to it: if they saw the tide coming in, the mothers would come up onto the bank, and the lambs would follow.

Salt marsh sheep fetched a premium at livestock markets, and it followed that putting sheep on the salt marsh was a common practice. 'My uncle had a horse and cart and every Sunday we'd all get in there and go to the sea wall, and collect the sheep, make sure everything was alright. We'd go down the lane, through two gates, then down to the sea wall, get up on the sea wall, then bring all the sheep up then, ready for shearing.

Saltmarsh sheep were in good demand, and fetched higher prices. So much so that at least one farmer had a go at selling his as 'Marsh Sheep' at market. When it was discovered that they were not the genuine article, he was called out. However, our Peterstone farmer could legitimately describe his sheep as salt marsh: 'The idea was to fatten the stock in the summer for the slaughterhouse. There'd be a gang of us, and we'd walk the lynches, which is where the edges of grass would drop off.'

We're chatting in his farmhouse kitchen, when he stands up to fetch something from the next room, and returns with two, leather-bound, three-inch thick volumes. He placed them in front of me: 'Take a look.' His grandfather's name is inscribed in large loops across the page of, what turns out to be, a blow-by-blow account of life on the farm in the first half of last century. 'In father's farm diaries, he writes about selling 98 lambs at market. And with the proceeds, he bought a 135 Massey tractor. Nowadays you'd probably have to sell a thousand sheep to get a tractor!' His own apprenticeship on the farm started when he was aged between four and five: 'I [was] only a nipper when I started helping bring the sheep in [for shearing]. It was a community thing, just like the old-fashioned days, helping each other out.

'We'd get the sheep in a pen here, and shear them in the shade. There'd be my father, probably my uncle Philip, three of them shearing. As kids we'd be catching them, rolling the wool; mother in here cooking food, then my cousins would come over.'

But times, he told me, have changed. The lynches, for example, are all gone 'because when they put the barrage in Cardiff, it eroded all the grass on our side. We've lost a lot of grazing out there. You could graze 50 meters out in places.'

A special Wharf Committee used to oversee access and permission to sea wall grazing, and there were sanctions for those who grazed sheep without permission. Marjorie Neal had grazing rights on the sea wall at her Rumney farm: 'Different farms down here have grazing rights on the sea wall, and we have four acres. It's only people with grazing rights [that] can put animals on the wall. Rumney Wharf had a committee, and they decided between them, a date the cattle could go on there, and the date they would have to come off, because they weren't on there through the winter months. It was roughly from about Easter through to December. Bulls and stallions were not allowed. The committee doesn't exist now, and we're the only ones with grazing on Rumney Great Wharf.'

Margaret Prosser's farm was just a field away from the sea wall at Peterstone, where their sheep were grazed: 'My husband's brother used to come up every Sunday from St Brides and sort them out. We were one of only a few farms with permission to graze sheep on the wharf. My brother-in-law'd be sitting in his horse and little trap, and then they'd go up to the sea wall to bring the sheep up. I remember on one occasion, the pony started kicking the bottom, and of course got out of the shaves, and left these four or five boys in the back, and it tipped backwards. But they were all fine, and the dog jumped out quick.'

Chapter 10

A lost crow, air like champagne, and the silent spring – Rumney to Cardiff

I'm reaching the end of my walk, and I have to prepare myself for entry back into normality. I haven't brushed my hair since I started, and like the Romans, I've only carried what I needed. I didn't choose the best of seasons, but in a way that has been a help. Physically, the walk has been easy. I'm fit and walk most days. I admit I was a wreck when I first set out at Chepstow. Losing a friend so suddenly has challenged me emotionally and mentally. But there has been an improvement. As I clocked the miles, the buffeting wind smoothed some of the edges. The soundscape has changed as much as the landscape. It's noisier here. I can hear construction work, trains, traffic, the motorway. It's not the cacophony I would have expected. In a way it's a welcome distraction.

Ron Dupe's childhood idyll at Rumney changed with the outbreak of war in 1939. Initially, there was great excitement in the air. 'As boys, we thought great! This is how boys think, you see?' When an air raid shelter was put up in the playground at Marshfield School, Ron changed his mind: 'This is serious.'

Stephanie Davies' family had an Anderson-type shelter, set in the vegetable garden at Upper Newton Farm, Rumney. Stephanie lived on a neat estate above Rumney. Her parents farmed near Rumney Wharf. 'We used to go in there at night-time when the air raid siren would sound, and stay there all night until morning. It was comfortable. I think my mother must have put bedding in there, because when we went in, we had something comfortable we could lie down on. And we just stayed there until the all clear went.'

During one of the worst night-time raids on Cardiff, Stephanie and her family could not reach their garden shelter, so they sheltered in the kitchen: 'We had the table in the middle, and there was a big chest on one side, a piano on the other, and my father had put a big thick plank across, and we were underneath that, with me, my sister and my mother and the dog.'

They heard a whistling sound as one bomb fell, hitting the ground near a farm building by the house. 'It landed on the other side of the barn near where the animals were. It was really loud, but the vibration from it was almost worse.'

In the silence that followed, Stephanie looked up: 'I can remember sitting inside, and I could see where the ceilings of the house had moved away, and we could see up through there. We did wonder if the house might collapse, so dad got us out, but because the blast had jammed the gate shut, we couldn't open it, so dad had to drag us over.'

In shock, the family hurried out of the farmhouse. 'We went across the yard and onto the road, and down to the next farm. We knocked on their door, and said "we've just been bombed", and they took us in. We stayed for a couple of nights.'

The reverberations affected the foundations of the house. It wasn't safe anymore. A couple of calves were killed, yet one cow, which had been chained up, was blown out of the barn. 'They found her wandering up the road the next morning, with the chain still round her neck, alive.'

Bombing by night gave way to day time raids, and Ron witnessed one daylight attack on Cardiff: 'The air raid siren went off, and we were all looking towards the dock, and saw a German plane come across, and drop nine bombs there.'

His excitement gave way to dismay, however, when the Luftwaffe lost him his pet crow.

'We had an ugly experience in 1941, January 2nd, when the Luftwaffe decided to pay us a visit, and put a hundred planes over Cardiff. They dropped flares that lit us up like day. There were tonnes of bombs floating down on parachutes.'

Two bombs fell in Rumney destroying several houses on New Road. 'And they dropped one directly behind what is the police station now – it was then the Country Maid Bakery. That one threw up so much mud. It was about 800 yards from our house. We had a large shed in the garage, and it knocked a hole in the roof there.

'At the time I had a pet crow, which couldn't fly (that was why I was looking after it). Then suddenly, when the bomb landed, it could fly again. It flew up through the hole! I was a bit upset about that.'

The Americans entered the war in December 1941, and communities up and down the country started to witness their arrival in preparation for D-Day. There must be families in Oregon, Texas and California with photos of the Levels, as they were in 1941, when their grand- or great-grandfathers were billeted here. They left quite an impression on local people, especially on those sweet-deprived youngsters under rationing.

These clean-cut American soldiers, or GIs, were popular, bearing gifts of chewing gum, chocolate and nylons. When Glyn Vincent attended Nash School, he reaped the benefits of having Americans stationed nearby. 'I was at school one day, and down where the power station is, there was an army camp for the Yanks. When they used to drive by in lorries, we shouted, "Any gum?" And they used to chuck some to us.'

Ivy James was less interested in gum than in dancing. American soldiers attended the regular hops in Chepstow:

'One had gold teeth. I remember all the Americans parked down Station Road, and my sister Iris used to go down on her little bike, and they used to say, "Can we have a ride?" So, she would let them get on and have a go, and then they would give her a tin of fruit and some gum. Mam was glad of that tin of fruit.'

GIs were stationed near Marjorie Neal's home at Rumney. 'A friend and I were playing opposite our house, and the gates for this sorting depot were about eight-foot-high, and the American soldiers threw chewing gum over the fence to us.' Marjorie was bemused: 'We had no idea what it was or what you were supposed to do with it, so of course they unwrapped it and showed us. "Take it out and put it in your mouth and chew it!" And that was our first taste of chewing gum.' But, as she told me, she also noted a somber side to the American's presence: 'Their base was called the Sea Transport Stores, and they had it for storing goods coming in from America, and being dispersed around this country and Europe, and for goods that were to be taken back to America. But that included the casualties of war: bodies'.

There is no longer any sign of bomb craters or American stores. The fields have long gone, and in their place is a vast urban sprawl. 'It was all just fields here,' said Stephanie Davies. 'That's where my father and uncle made hay in the 1930s.' Stephanie's story is common to many others. Fields once used for haymaking, are now home to housing, fast food empires and out-of-town shopping malls. Spytty Park is a monument to shopping, yet this was rich farmland within living memory. It is where a young Glynn Vincent used to come for the raw materials for thatching: 'We used to go haymaking up at Spytty Park, and go all the way up to Lliswerry to get the reeds for thatching the ricks, by the side of the railway line. You'd have a hook and cut the reeds off, gather them in a bundle. Then you'd put your arm around them, put them on a cart and fetch them back, and put them on the top of the rick.'

Another significant change has been the way the reens are cleared with heavy machinery. I first met John Southall on the side of a reen, in a new housing development on the Wentlooge Level. He's supervising a digger driver, clearing debris and silt from the water channel. It's his job to remain vigilant, and keep these reens clear, running and functioning. He has a team of men and heavy machinery, but it wasn't always thus.

A man in a cap with a pushbike and tools strapped to the crossbar was usually all it took, as Kath Johnson reminded me back in Goldcliff. The worker was a familiar and reassuring sight, and often on first name terms with locals: 'Years ago the men used to trim all the reens by hand. They used a hook. They be doing it by tractor now, but then they did it all by hand. We used to see them and have a talk to them. Alf Stevens was one of them, Bert Stevens, Billy England, John Cox were the others. They'd all be out trimming the reens. If there was a blockage, they used a big old rake.'

Things didn't always go to plan, however, as Sue Waters recalled: 'I remember for most of my younger life, there was a group of old gentlemen who were employed by the River Board. They used to clean the reens out with their billhooks, and their variously named instruments, and they spent the entire summer and winter doing it, and you saw the difference in the summer. They kept those reens clear, far better than they do with machinery today.' But one day they felled a favourite tree of Sue's. 'They cut off my Whitsun Boss tree and I was very cross! It was a very beautiful tree with creamy flower heads blooming out at Whitsuntide. It had grown too far over the watercourse, so they cut it back.'

Robert Higgins also enjoyed watching men like Bill Giles at work on the reens: 'He had a big, long-handled hook and a rake, and he used to have those tied to his cross bar. He cleaned all the sluices and regulated the flow of the water, and kept all the reeds out of the reen. Today it's just a tractor in the field, a great big bucket thing that cleans them out.'

Wooden barriers were employed to control irrigation on the Levels. Who received water and who did not, however, could give rise to arguments. Ken Reece told me of one incident: 'There was a chap from Redwick, who used to come and take the boards out, or put boards in, to control water flow. He was employed by the Drainage Board. It was never a very easy job, because people up at Bishton always wanted the water gone, and then perhaps other people elsewhere wanted to keep the water. I can remember one man from Bishton, and he always had an axe with him, threatening to chop the boards out.'

I spoke to one Rumney farmer who, while he understood the difficulties of modern drainage, nevertheless hankered back to the old, non-bureaucratic ways. 'Going back fifty or sixty years ago there was an old boy, Mr Williams, and you only had to say you needed to get water to a particular place, and in the next couple of days, and he would put the boards in to make sure the water would back-fill up. He was a bit of a farmer from the other end of the Moors, at Ty Mawr. He'd been on it for so many years, and he knew exactly what water would go where. He would block off at a certain point, and that would back-fill to neighbour A; or if neighbour B wanted water somewhere else, he could do it.' Another ditcher took it upon himself to ration the water as equitably as he could: 'It wasn't a matter of ringing up Joe Bloggs and getting permission, he would put a pump in a certain place, put boards in a ditch, and put clay behind the boards to stop them leaking, and pump water then to you. So that was a big advantage to us as farmers, because it meant we could fall back on him. But it's all automated now.'

The first motorway edged onto the Levels with the opening of the Severn Bridge in 1967. Pam Robertson had a close-up look in the early 1960s, when the motorway tore a first strip across this part of South Wales. Her husband ran a fleet of JCBs working on its construction. We talked at her home in Marshfield: 'I can claim to have driven my car the wrong way on the motorway. I used to deliver fuel and wages in my pickup truck to the JCB drivers working on it. There was no traffic because it hadn't even opened then, so I drove the wrong way down the M4. Not many people can say that.

'Beyond Newport, and through the tunnels and, I think, to the Coldra, we were probably working there for about two years. On Tuesdays my job was to go around all the sites, collect the timesheets from the drivers, give them fuel or hydraulic oil if they needed it, carry a couple of spare wheels in case they needed them too. And my Thursday job was to work out the wages, and then on the Friday deliver them around the sites on the motorway.'

In July 2014, Economy Minister Edwina Hart of the Welsh Government, gave the go-ahead for a highly-contraversial 14-mile, six-lane stretch of the M4, to relieve a bottleneck on the M4 between Magor and Castleton, to the cost of around £1 billion.

There was uproar, as people realized it would cause untold damage to this historic landscape. When the Welsh government scrapped the proposal in the summer of 2019, it was already too late for the corncrake, the numbers of which have dropped dramatically. Terry Theobald told me how, when in 1964 he and his family moved into their new home, Rogiet was 'like a proper village. I can remember look-ing out, and there was fields, as far as you could see. In the spring, you would hear this high-pitched scream, and you could hear the corncrakes. But then the original M4 came through the whole lot of it, and that was the end of the corncrakes. I haven't heard them since.'

His childhood playground has gone, and Ron Dupé's eyes mist over as he talks about his boyhood. 'I am so old,' he tells me, 'that I don't have any enemies; I've outlived them all!' He is a sprightly 94 and has been married for 62 years. He lives in a light-filled apartment in Porthcawl, with views across the bay. But between the wars, he lived in rural Rumney. 'For a child, Rumney was paradise, an absolute paradise. Meant for youngsters. It was beautiful because there was only two main roads, and there were very old cottages there.' Eventually, he says, 'one by one, they were pulled down and rebuilt as new houses.'

Ron remembers river adventures: 'My friend Bill and I had a little boat, and we used to sail up and down the Rhymney river. I was Tom Sawyer and he was Huckleberry Finn. We used to come home covered in mud very often.' The two boys nearly came to grief, not on the tide, but in the river silt: 'My friend was the same age as me, but he was a very strong lad, and as we were going down to the boat I got stuck and couldn't move. The mud had me. "Bill, I can't move!" He put his arm out and it was like a rod of iron. And I just hung on to him and pulled myself out.'

Traditionally farmed landscapes like these were rich in wildlife, which is partly why the Severn Estuary to the south of the Levels, was designated as a Special Protection Area for rare and vulnerable birds. It's also a Special Area of Conservation for threatened saltmarsh habitats, and for species including river and sea lamprey *(Petromyzon marinus)*, twaite shad *(Alosa fallax)*, salmon and eel. And the River Usk, which divides the Wentloog and Caldicot

Levels as it flows from Newport into the Severn Estuary, also support habitats of international significance.

The Levels are also home to a wide variety of birds, particularly waders and waterfowl, the dunlin, shoveller, little egret, little grebe and more. Robert Higgins, however, remembered the goldfinches nesting in his family orchard, long before the reserve arrived: 'My brother and I used to play football in the orchard, and my grandmother would shout, "You'll knock the apples off the trees" and chase us around the house. We had an apple tree and a pear tree just in front of the kitchen window. I can always remember the pear tree, because we used to get goldfinches building nests in it. I can hear them now twittering in the trees. It was lovely in the morning listening to them.' Like many others on the Levels, he has noted the decline in birdlife 'We used to get a lot of bullfinches and chaffinches, but the bullfinches, we've lost a lot of them. You just don't see them so much anymore.'

Monica Howells at Goldcliff has noticed changes too along the seashore. 'When I was small, there were large flocks of lapwings around here, and partridges too. You would walk down the field and they'd take off and make you jump. When I was a child, in the cold of winter, the gulls used to come and land in the field by us.' Living in such close proximity to the birds enabled Monica to read their behaviour: 'If it was going to snow, they sort of had this moaning voice on them. And the peewits [lapwings] used to come too, if it was going to snow. They just seemed to know. They used to nest in the grips, because they could run down the fields to the sea wall. But they were awful because they used to dive bomb us. Another thing I really miss are the sparrows. There used to be flocks of them. When I fed the chickens, the sparrows used to follow me in a flock. But these days you only see about a dozen. We still have a few skylarks though. We used to love seeing them in the sky when we went to the sea wall, and hear them singing.'

The healthy wild bird populations of the past, came with farming practices that were gentler than current ones. 'In those days we had quite a bit of wildlife,' recalled Ron Perry, who remembers the natural conservation methods of the small-scale farmer: 'We had no fertiliser. I started mowing at 14 years of age with two horses. When I was rolling the first field with the horse, my father made me keep three foot away from the grips, because that's where the birds nested, and he didn't want me to run over them.

'So, we kept at least a yard out from them. He was very concerned, [even though] the peewits were plentiful then. I mean, when we were working in the field, they'd dive bomb you, and they'd shout and scream at you.'

Ron was always careful not to disturb nests: 'When we were mowing one year in the eight acres at home, father left a piece in the middle of the field, about the size of this room. And I said to him, "What did you leave that for?" He said, "There's a partridge sitting in the middle of there." And he left it until she hatched, then went over with a scythe and he only cut it then.'

Just as Monica used to 'read' the birds, Ron's father used to observe the skylark as his forecaster. 'On a nice summer morning, you could hardly see them, and they would eventually go out of sight, but you could still hear them. And my father used to say, "The higher he is, the finer the weather will be." He was always right.'

Ron's father also relied on local flora for his weather forecasting: 'He used to come out in the morning, and look at the little scarlet pimpernel flower, and if it was wide open he would say, "It will be a fine day today," but if it closed up, he would say, "That's it, it's gonna rain."'

Ron also noted changes in weather patterns. 'We used to get colder winters then you see, but better summers. In the winter you'd get the wild geese coming over from the north, down this way, and dad would say, "We're in for a cold spell now," and about a fortnight later we'd had our cold spell and they were going back. We could tell the time by them. It was a different way of life, see?'

Searching for birds' nests was a popular childhood pursuit in the old days. Children knew which birds nested where, and when, and could anticipate their return after a winter away. Sue Waters went searching at Nash: 'We didn't take the eggs, but we knew where all the nests were. And if you were down the field, there were wasps' and bees' nests. And we had adders – we had long grass in one of the orchards - and father used to say, "now don't you go down there or the snakes will bite you." And of course, we didn't listen.' Sue was taken aback one morning, when she found a dead snake woven into the branches of a tree. It was an adder: 'Obviously it had been killed, and my father had placed it there as a warning to us.'

Kath Johnson went bird nesting with her father. It was also an excuse for him to propagate his garden roses: 'We used to walk miles looking for bird nests. It was lovely. But we never took any eggs out of the nest, you'd just walk, and he'd say, "listen", and you'd hear tweeting and sometimes you'd see the little babies in the nest. It was just lovely doing that. We'd be walking around the hedges, looking for bird nests and then he would find the best dog rose briar. It'd have to be a thick one, and he'd tie a little bit of raffia around it. And then he would go and dig it up later on in the autumn.' Her father would take a cutting from one of his favourite garden roses, and graft it onto the rose wood stock, protecting the graft with a layer of clay held in place with raffia. 'Then he'd graft it in the autumn, and they'd be his standard roses, dog briars. Lovely they were.'

In July 2021, Julie James, Welsh Minister for Climate Change, said that the location of the Gwent Levels made them vulnerable to encroachment by built development and infrastructure. 'As part of our heightened response to the climate change and nature emergencies, I am keen to ensure that areas like the Gwent Levels are better protected and managed for the future,' she said. Many Levellers would agree.

Back in 1962 Rachel Carson published her book *Silent Spring*, a warning about the environmental consequences of using pesticides. Ron reflected on how the silent spring hit the Levels: 'I remember walking over the railway line, where the steelworks is now, and seeing yellow hammers, reed warblers and corn buntings – they were everywhere. There was wildlife everywhere bird-wise, because it was perfect habitat, you see?' But, he added, 'the thing I used to enjoy listening to most of all was the skylarks. I haven't heard a skylark for 50 years.'

Acknowledgements

I am indebted to the people of the Moors, who have contributed their personal experiences, welcomed me into their homes and fortified me with copious cups of tea and fruit cake. It's been a joy. Thanks also to the Living Levels Team, Chris Harris, Alison Boyes, Sian Lloyd, Gavin Jones and Elinor Meloy for their unwavering help and support. They have done the Levels and this project justice. The project was made possible thanks to the National Heritage Lottery Funding. Thank you to RSPB Cymru for sharing some of their older interviews. Special mention also to my editor Bill Laws, whose help, support, and friendship I'm really grateful for. So many people helped me along the way. Not all their stories appear in this book, but they are part of the public record and available at People's Collection Wales.

There are so many people to thank, most importantly those who kindly agreed to be interviewed. They are: Professor Martin Bell, Bev Cawley, Paul Cawley Cath Davies, Philip Davies, Stephanie Davies, Ron Dix, Bob and Cherry Dowsell, Ron Dupé, John Evans, Ray Evans, Robert Evans, Mike George, Tony and Chris George, Margaret and Julie Gutteridge, Mary Hahn, Douglas Howells, Monica Howells, David Hurn, Ivy James, Kath Johnson, Howard Kyte, Brian Lane, Dr Mark Lewis, Mike Mazzoleni, Martin Morgan, Marjorie Neal, Jan Preece, Roley and Ann Price, Andrew Prosser, Margaret Prosser, Ken Reece, Ruth Richardson, Professor Steve Rippon, Pam Robertson, Tony Rodriguez, Terry Rooney, Gordon and Linda Shears, John Southall, Val Southall, John and Judith Smalls, Terry Theobald, Iris Theobald, Arthur and Anne Thomas, Bob Trett, Ann and Glynn Vincent, Neville Waters MBE, Sue

Waters, Ed Watts, Adrian Williams, Jim Worrington, and Coral Yates. Thanks also to Newport Library, Chepstow Library, Glamorgan Archives, and Newport Museum and Art Gallery.

Glossary

Back-fen: traditionally the wettest part of the Levels and was the last to be properly drained.

Cast or throw a ditch: removing the silt from a ditch and cleaning it back to the original profile.

Causeway: a raised passage across low-lying lands (e.g. The Causeway, Undy).

Gout: a channel that takes water through a structure to the sea, a sluice or floodgate, or a covered drain.

Grips: Small open furrows or ditches, especially for carrying off water.

Lynch: a small inland cliff. Lynches is the local name for the mud cliff on Rumney Great Wharf.

Pill: A Severn Estuary term for a tidal creek, the section of a watercourse seaward of an outfall or gout.

Reaping and scouring: These maintenance tasks ensure that reens are kept free of vegetation and silt.

Reens: Large open ditches or drains that are the primary feature of a complex drainage system that conveys surface water to the sea.

Saltmarsh: A marsh overflowed or flooded by the sea. Often this can be used for summer grazing when the tides are generally lower.

Sewer: An artificial watercourse for draining marshy land and carrying off surface water into a river or the sea. Sewers are the collective name for any type of watercourse on the Levels.

Stank: A stank can be a pond or a pool, a ditch of slowly-moving water, a dam to hold back water or a weir. Many stanks are inhabited by moorhens, known locally as the 'stankhen.'

Tide flap or tide gate: A flapped opening through which surface water flows towards the sea on the ebb-tide, but closes against the flood-tide to prevent tidal ingress inland.

Wet fence: A reen or ditch along a field boundary whose water ensures that livestock are kept within the field.

Wharf: A flat meadow, especially low-lying grazing lands along the Severn Estuary. Sometimes referred to as salt wharf or fresh wharf depending on its position relative to the sea wall.

Index